The Alchemy Spoon
Issue 7: Summer 2022

The Alchemy Spoon
Issue 7: Summer 2022

Editors
Roger Bloor
Vanessa Lampert
Mary Mulholland

A poetry magazine with a special interest in 'new phase' poets

Design and production
Clayhanger Press

Typeset in Times New Roman

Poetry Submissions
Our submission window is next open from 1ˢᵗ – 31ˢᵗ October 2022

Please read the submissions guidelines on the final page
Submissions are through the website
www.alchemyspoon.org

Cover Images

Front Cover: *Double exposure of flooded subway*, photograph by Alex Harford

Back Cover: *Imagination: Tranklement*, photograph by Dawn Jutton of her
exhibition piece

On foot
I had to cross the solar system
before I found the first thread of my red dress.
I sense myself already.
Somewhere in space hangs my heart,
shaking in the void, from it stream sparks
into other intemperate hearts.

Edith Sodergran

Contents

Editorial

'a breathtaking stellar nursery called the Carina nebula is so rich in detail that researchers could discern bubbles, cavities and jets blasting out of newborn stars, along with hundreds more stars they had never seen before'. Ian Sample, *The Guardian*, 12 July, 2022[1]

As I write this editorial, spectacular images are hurtling back from the far reaches of the cosmos which are likely to re-define our notion of outer space. When we arrived at an agreed theme of 'space' for issue 7, I envisaged the 'final frontier', 'outer space' kind of space. I anticipated being invited, via the poems about to flood our way, to hurtle through endless silent darkness ricocheting between planets, freed from gravity, dangerously surrounded by words I would have to google. I would be required to think once more about outer space not having any edges – at all – there aren't any. This poetry might both enlighten and tether me.

In his poem 'The Indian Rope Trick' Tim Love writes 'don't be afraid of the dark –/ it's space, not night/ the moon won't follow you.' Reassurance is perhaps the foundation stone of rapport. Essentially the power of poetry lies in its reader being convinced to forget everything else and jump in. Come with me, says the poet speaker, I know the way, and it will be an impoverished event in your absence. It won't take long. After all this is a poem, a smallish thing. Miles Gibson echoes this sentiment in his poem 'Comeback'. 'Impossible! As the size of our galaxy/ that I should choose to be apart from you'.

A poet succeeds by the creation of a feeling of intimacy between the reader and themselves. They must convince the reader to take their hand and move through the poem with its speaker as a guide. This act of decreasing the space between poet and reader carries the potential for a poem to be experienced as a shared sanctuary. An effective poem convinces the reader they are not alone; a brief respite, sometimes antidote to the psychological space of loneliness.

Don Paterson describes the creative opportunity to write poetry: 'Our poetic meditations allow us to enter a space where new and original connections can be forged beyond language, and then find their linguistic incarnation at its very limits.'[2] On page 59 you will find Mary Mulholland's interview with Caroline Bird, a poet of dizzying feats of linguistic athleticism. To commit to being in the space of one of Caroline Bird's poems is something akin to being in an immersive theatre production. You have no idea what will

---

[1]   https://www.theguardian.com/science/2022/jul/12/nasa-publishes-flurry-of-images-from-james-webb-space-telescope
[2] Don Paterson, *The Poem*, Faber & Faber, 2018

happen next but you are committed to stay until the white space at the end of the poem tells you it is over.

Poetry also offers the opportunity to play with the space afforded on the page. Tim Relf's poem 'Lunch, then' places the words '2m' and 'apart' away from each other, the visual field offering a pleasing interpretation of what the words say, with the characters of the poem's narrative placed beneath in the centre of the page: 'The two of us sat; sanitised under her maple tree'.

Pat Winslow is our featured poet for issue 7. You will find her poems on pages 24 and 25, with a link to a video of her reading and discussing her poems on page 69. 'Somewhere, a lark is threading/ a silver monologue/ and the wren is winding itself/ like a pocket watch in the grass.'

In an extended Personal View on page 50 Professor Al Filreis reflects on the creation of a poetry course in virtual space from his experiences directing the open online poetry course on Modern & Contemporary American Poetry called *ModPo*.

Thank you to everyone who sent us poems for this issue. Without you we are nothing but **space** [*noun*]: **an empty area that is available to be used**.[3]

Vanessa Lampert

---

[3] https://dictionary.cambridge.org/dictionary/english/space

Attention

On works by James Cowie

He always started with the eyes, building
the rest of the face and body from there

and you see with what deliberation
he tried to see what would happen when this
body (entirely and exclusively
itself) was juxtaposed with that (ditto).

Against a backdrop both interior
and exterior the air-raid warden
holding his pencil like a cigarette
sees something slightly higher than himself

just beyond the frame, blue fabric falling
from the laps of two school girls, self-contained
and looking across each other before
the statuette of a discus thrower

they pay as little heed to as the leaves
falling there outside the classroom window
during the drawing class, skin and hair tones
against those of paper, cloth, wood and stone,

smoke, drapes the wind catches, a bird in flight,
the horse a huntsman rides, fields, trees, hedgerows,
the dry summer road turning near the farm
and the four seated at table somewhat

awkwardly, three happed inside their jackets,
the men looking left, the younger woman
directly at us while, arms and neck bare,
the older woman toys with her pinkie.

Then the late still lives, mirror and maquette,
the tanagra's arm covering its eyes.

Ken Cockburn

Hangers

Mechanical clamour threshes the air;
hydraulic coughs, thick and insistent,
hack my space. I sit before a machine

that spews plastic hangers, two at a time,
every ten seconds. A small spot on each,
still molten hot, for hooks to be added

by hand – the tricky part. It's a blind reach.
Spike-entangled metal stabs my fingers.
I fit the hooks. Will they stay? Successes

hang on the rail behind me, rejects lie
in a cardboard box. Some try to fool me,
sway for a while, then fall. Timing is all.

Annie Morris

Caesura

Between cup and lip,   the distance of a slip;
        the radio's hiss as you pass beneath the bridge;
the break   on the windscreen   of the splattering of the rain;
        the gap,   as you step   from the platform to the train.

These are the signs of the permanent pause,
        of the stopping of the clock,   of the tick   with no tock.
If you're not sure of much,   then be sure of this:
                one day   the caesura will not cease.

The mute blue screen of the terminal fault;
        the brokendown car   rolling to a halt
                in the still dark silence of a country lane;
        in the middle of the tunnel,   the stationary train.

These are the warnings of the permanent pause,
        of the stopping of the clock,   of the tick   with no tock.
If you're not sure of much,   then be sure of this;
                one day   the comma   will be a full-stop.

The flutter of your heart,   like the flicker of a light,
        when you wake   in a sweat   in the dead of the night,
and you listen for the thief,   and you can't fight the feeling
                that he's coming up the stairs,   as you stare at the ceiling.

These are the signs of the permanent pause,
        of the stopping of the clock,   of the tick   with no tock.
If you're not sure of much,   then be sure of this:
                one day   the caesura,

Martin Yates

Rehearsal notes for first contact

Your approach should be cautious,
focus your consciousness
into your fingertip
as it crosses the compound eye
of countless screens.

To the actor opposite,
the whorl of your friction ridges
may be seen as a metaphor:
of isobars describing a storm or,
more likely, the unknown.

Stanislavski says the fingertip
is the eye of the body.
Gently extend your finger
to convey human curiosity:
our yearning towards.

Know the interstellar audience
will barely be breathing,
clenched by the realisation
of what players already know:
one touch can double the world.

Peter Kenny

All at Sea

Bleached decking,
black iron, air.

Sunday afternoon
walk on water.

A sudden skyline
where it stops.

Look back at houses
built on sand.

Eat a pink bouffant
of sugar on a stick.

Crack sweet glaze,
bite soft white pulp.

Drop lines to catch
venomous weaver fish,

crabs that clamber
on each other

in a bucket,
warm specks of jelly

inside a husk,
stalk eyes, spine feet.

As earth pulls water
round her shoulders,

tip the bucket over the rail,
roll up lines and hooks,

walk to Macari's for a bus
that will get us home

before lights go on
all the way to the end.

Chris Hardy

12

The glove marriage

for Anne Thomas

She marries by proxy, whispers her vows
to an empty glove sent by a man
on the other side of the globe.

The glove smells of tobacco and dogs.
It bears his hand's imprint, the creases
where his fingers grasp the horse's reins.

She slips her fingers into its looseness,
her ring catches a thread. She thinks
of his large strong hand meeting

the right glove's waiting sheath, the glove
he has and holds from this day forward.
She sips her spiced red wine.

Mary Robinson

Breakfast in Mattapoisett

The day is lemon yellow.
Chopin fills your rooms, Hokusai's wave
breaks inside its blue frame.

As you pour coffee,
a vine of steam climbs between us,
vanishing, leaving me your face

flushed with our sleep,
the hungry spaces inside us brimming.
You draw me a map outlining the way home,

your pencil precise, a labyrinth
of squares at your command.
Under the table our laps share a shadow.

Jeri Onitskansky

Safe Space

You left your picture behind,
crumpled in the black toybox,
scribbled over with red crayon.
A winged lady with horns,
holding a scythe, grinning.

They promised not to touch
the toys you played with today.
A sharp stack of stickle bricks,
hard plastic horses tangled
in a knot of string.

Two floor fans hang their heads
scanning the mud-brown floor
for secrets you may have dropped.
A smear of daylight seeps through
misted glass. The room looks out

over a wall painted white.
A lone plant straggles
a wire trellis tacked to brick.
Slatted blinds pencil light
on the slate-grey couch.

A black plastic protector
hides marks from small shoes.
The only splash of colour
an emerald green sign
a boy running for the exit.

Judith Wozniak

My address is my baggage

The interview went fine,
yet I didn't get the job,
they said I did well,
as I know I could,
but I was denied even getting a try,
even a slight chance,
to even glimpse the boss,
they said that they understand,
but my address is my baggage.

I went to school and paid attention,
The teacher said that I work well,
listen well,
attentive,
dress well,
well mannered,
spoke well,
but my address,
Oh, my address is my baggage.

I was born there,
my parents live there
my brothers too,
my best friends,
but the interviewing panel listen to the news,
I know,
The questions they asked,
the happenings on my street,
the expression on their face.
My street was a concern,
now I'm paying,
my address is my baggage.

On this little island,
on this little rock,
where can I go?
Where no one knows my street,
the police tape,
How can I erase it?
The news,

the blood,
It was all in the news,
my address is my baggage,
how long should this journey last?

Dennis Williams

Shauny Bubble

I see you in Nivea pink lather
as I wash your granddaughter's little limbs
like you washed mine when I was *muddy knees*

I see you in sea foam on Weybourne beach
walks we never did together   I see
you rise in lager pints we never shared

I see you erupt in boiling water
as I make 2am tea in your *Best*
Dad mug   I see you trapped in a spirit
level still reminding me I'm not straight

I never asked you why *Shauny Bubble*
was your life-long nickname   maybe *Bubble*
was your first word   your first teddy   maybe
everybody knew you'd float briefly   burst

James McDermott

Last Summer

I once cut my father's hair as he sat pliantly
in a weathered deck chair overlooking a line
of spindly hemlocks in the Carolina mountains.

It was such an intimate act, the lifting of his
silvered strands, peppered here and there,
guiding the scissors tenderly around his ears,

bits of silver and gray feathering off into
the breeze, into the trees, my hands smoothing
and combing into place the shaggy tendrils

at the nape of his neck. It was the last summer
of his life, the summer before his good heart
skipped and stuttered, dipping him to his knees

on the kitchen mat back home, where he tipped
sideways and out of this world.

Bridget Ramsey

A Good Hiding

In the airing cupboard, igniting eyes
kindle his world.

A tin shelf is the brow of his ship,
in the hold a stash of gold and silver:
clocks and watches, broken springs, buckles,
razors emptied of their blades,
animal bones.

He flicks the shelf and it rings,
his ears become the gobs of beasts eating noise,
his skin tingles,
glowing coins spill over casket rims,
he bangs his heels,
clocks wake up and watches
tick the beat of his heart.

Beneath his hair, a birthmark itches,
picks up the squeak of Dad's belt
sliding through its loops.

Janet Dean

Comeback

Setting your secretive face far, far away,
you leave the car for another school day.
'See you…soon', tailing off,
as 'soon' is not tonight or even tomorrow.
Pack ladened, you break into a bumpy run.
Like some human airbag,
I lurch to inflate around you.

This term your topic is Space.
I remember writing:
I struggle to fasten your dress,
when once I struggled to loosen your mother's.
And each night, I'd check on you and think:
Impossible! As the size of our galaxy,
that I could choose to be apart from you.

Today I will customize a pencil case.
A ruler that strengthens the spine,
A Tippex apologist to whitewash.
Then, out with the felt tip lightsabers,
and we'll slice into the future,
Rey and old Skywalker, on a comeback,
bright waves blue, green and gold.

Miles Gibson

Migratory – Going Home with Bruegel

I always forget
that Bruegel's hunters
walk in snow.
And that they must be cold.
The hunters walk, heads heavy,
towards the town below.
They've caught one hare
and are bringing it home.
Home, where people skate
on Lowlands lakes
bordered by Alpine heights.
Bruegel's landscape
is of two places, remembered
and imagined.

I walk to the end of my non-native
street, the edge of a wood.
Trees slope to the bank of a river.
I stand still for a moment
and savour the vista
I see through
the network of branches,
with cows and meadows
low down, across the water.
Budding leaves veil the view.
As I observe the
familiar landscape
the skaters return. They begin
to glide in the distance.

Marian de Vooght

The Hanged Man

After Leonard Baskin's woodcut 1955

When flesh falls away
the sinews and the bones preside
turning slowly on a rope
pendant from the nearest star.

The hanged man lets the wind blow through
to clean away his human form
and leave behind this cage of air
delicate as a leaf, dried in patterns
of old sap and long-trapped sun.

Martin Rieser

How Shall We Bury Our Dead?

The people keep coming and people keep dying.
On the edge of the camp the cemetery's full.

We lay our loved ones on top of each other.
How else can we bury them when there's no room?

How shall we tend them? Who will cleanse them?
Who will spread balm when there's none to be had?

Who will clothe them and beat drums of mourning
when all that we have has been left behind?

Who will visit the man who died longing
for the touch of a loved one, the land of his birth?

Who knows he is here? How will they find him?
He arrived with no passport. Without papers he's no one.

We go, after dark, when the city is sleeping.
We must bury our dead wherever we can.

And now there's a rumour – a woman in black
who comes past our fence, a woman whose baby

was buried at dawn will reopen the grave
so one of our mothers can bury her son.

In silence and stealth, the kindness of strangers
the gift of a home for a child who had none.

Pat Winslow

The Season of Burning Heather

The day the clocks change
and the wind drops

the loch is transformed
to sky and machair.

Smoke plumes gently
against pale blue.

I've put the washing out
left it to hang in the flavoured air

so I can wear the memory
next to my skin.

Somewhere, a lark is threading
a silver monologue

and the wren is winding itself
like a pocket watch in the grass.

The pulsing wingbeat of a goose
copies itself across water.

Closer still, the papery sound
of a bee disturbs a daffodil.

Pat Winslow

Portrait of my grandfather as a crop-duster plane

My grandfather's name was Orlik: in Polish this means *eagle*,
as in white eagle, as in soaring, national symbol.
Except the only thing he ever had named after him
was a crop-duster plane, a present from his comrades
in the Socialist Party, for services to the State
as director of Warsaw Domestic Airport. I remember
seeing it in the newspaper; a squat, undignified thing
less like my grandfather and more like
the mushrooms he made a point of picking. Mostly silent,
he rose from the porch and without warning
took flight to the forest, returning with just the one
fat cep, or penny-bun, porcino, *prawdziwek*
loosely translated as 'righteous one'
which he brought back with ceremony
to my grandmother, who clapped one brawny arm over his shoulder
Misio! before turning to us, *He's not done that in years*
And that's how I'll remember him: his back disappearing,
nose dipping as he hovered then dived
low to the forest floor.

Alexandra Williams

The Indian Rope Trick

There's nothing to it really.
Just keep climbing.
Don't look down at the words.
When you pass the clouds
don't be afraid of the dark -
it's space, not night;
the moon won't follow you.
Keep climbing until you're too far away
to hear applause or crying.
Even after years they'll be waiting,
thinking you're going to come back.

Tim Love

Best Thing Ever

is football in the snow by moonlight.

You could say tacos
but football in the snow by moonlight
crunches harder.

You could say kids
but football in the snow by moonlight
never says it hates you
and is also kids.

You could say beer
or strawberry sundaes the night you met your wife
but football in the snow by moonlight is colder.

You could say love
but football in the snow by moonlight
is warmer.

Frank Brunner

Lunch, then

2m   apart
          the two of us sat; sanitised under her maple tree.

Finding joy in the little things, that's the secret, she said,
as she had so many times –
my mum,
85 years old:
seed catalogue by her side, plate perched on lap, coatless in the sudden sunshine
and watching her squeeze out the last of the Tommy K then spoon on the mustard – a first,
    then a second, huge dob – I understood. Finally, I understood.

The little things, I tell myself   2 years on,

trying to remember what it felt like: to eat hotdogs outdoors in November.

Tim Relf

the best years are the ones you create space

you ask me what of the past
year I want to burn

and my first thought is
the songlessness

I want to be part of a chanting
crowd again

I want unheard-of melody
and harmonies

to find all the buried music
inside of me and pass it around

to strangers

Laura Theis

Fossils Lodged on the Coast

                                        imprints of absence
                nestled ciphers
                        accidental documentation
of existence
                                inhabiting the archive
                                    watchful guardians
                these hooded ghosts
            performing mournful hum

dark eyes peering
            from beneath   and
        from before
                        rows of diligent
                        record-keepers
                        rotted into rock

                                    stone-cold impressions
                of life
        speak
            to what   will come

Catherine Redford

This sky

By tomorrow I will have forgotten this sky
and the way the pigeons hang in veer like motes
in space swept out by the wind
as the train spools past, like the swoop
in a city of a knocked-down building
(the sudden hush in the scape);
the sense that there is nothing
meant to mean here – that slowing un-sense;
the open hand that's just cast up
a clutch of stars, or grit.

Sam Bootle

Sandy Point

1938, post-hurricane

Sandy Point is a 35-acre barrier island in Little Narragansett Bay, USA.

i.
This place is the same and not the same.
All the trees are dead, tossed
like jackstraws.
                        I came here
because New London burned, because
rescue efforts in Mystic Bridge found live fish
and crabs in the Noyes' kitchen drawers.

I walk among the dead forest.
Wood shifts at my feet,
as if I were a ghost. As if
I were a hurricane.

ii.
I came looking for something of me.

What I found: wet timber. Shallow water teeming.
Dead fish and the body of a dog.

iii.
This is not the sand
I walked on yesterday. Plovers
sit on the stumps. And, just there,
beach grass stretches first shoots
into the light air.

Jennifer A. McGowan

At No Point Does She Look Back

At the beach, my granddaughter,
not yet three, runs full tilt, naked
to the wide, low-tide water.

We adults park on sand,
lean back on hands under sun,
expand, watch her go.

Narrow-eyed, I gauge her speed,
judge the moment to begin
my steady run to shoreline.

I reach her at wave break,
her gleeful feet swirling in foam,
my right hand there, ready.

Tamsin Cottis

Credo

I believe in that line that lingers
beneath the title. Before the first word.
The space where meaning and potential mingle.

I trust in the metaphor, that lives on
long after the poet makes shape
out of stillness.

I have faith in the new image
that catches the heart
to resolve something unsaid.

To lean in to the poetry
is to know there is no cure
for this love. Let words be my witness.

I believe in the white silence
rising beyond the last inked point,
where everything waits,

and wants to be understood.

Kate Oldfield

Sitting

in the stateroom late September
he stares ahead at the yellow wall.

He hopes this portrait will elevate
him to an elder statesman.

The hand that signed declarations
of war lies sleeping in his lap.

She sees a balding man, thin smile,
trapped, like an upturned beetle.

Fokkina McDonnell

Sixty Years A Shed

Stacked high with spare parts
that might've come in handy,
innards of gramophones, defunct TVs
from table to rafters, behind its swollen door –
we cleared the shed that Dad built.

Walls of rose-red Abersychan brick,
a cottage window, corrugated roof,
plumbed-in brass tap, Bakelite switch
he'd wired to a naked bayonet bulb
which lit the shed that Dad built.

The mangle Mam turned each washing day,
the boiler where her *pudds* were cooked,
the iron last where Granddad tapped in
tacks and segs to his single shoe –
had witnessed work in the shed Dad built.

Spider webs swung between the beams,
lawn mower blades would drop their load,
and Joey tortoise wintered in a box
wrapped in straw – but never woke up
when spring warmed the shed that Dad built.

Was its roof asbestos? Did the concrete floor crack?
Best not return… so I'll never know
if new owners chose to make their mark
and filled a skip with rose-red rubble
knocked from the shed that Dad built.

Janet Lancaster

Far from the Dance

Every time
that music slips me back.

I should have held your hand

reached out across our
small forbidden space

our formal, absurd ice.

I couldn't speak;
you never heard.

Unplayed symphony:
this deafening rain.

Sue Lewis

Laika, you must understand

Laika was the first animal to orbit the Earth. Before lift-off a technician kissed her nose and wished her bon voyage, knowing that she would not survive the flight.

From the first moment
your milky eye slid a blind crescent
into the warm horizon of your mother,
it would always end this way.

We chose you, the bones and shiver of you
on the Moscow streets:
the oil-blue orbs of your eyes
planets we might one day visit,

the tilt of your listening, that way you had
of wagging your whole being,
and those perfect claws, almost translucent,
pared from the Earth's shadow.

We pinned you to the stars
so many miles away we could only imagine
your panic at the seismic roar
rushing past your window.

We measured it, of course,
tracked your frantic heart inside
its shuddering cage,
mapped your fear from peak to peak

as furious needles scribbled mountains,
fizzing constellations.
No one mentioned that the heat
was rising.

And as you died, still trusting our return,
desperate for the door to open,
two thousand miles away
we watched your last slow exhalation.

Gentle *Kudryavka, Zhuchka,*
we shall always remember your pale light
trembling like shook foil
in that dreadful sky.

Jane Lovell

Stars

Ten thousand stars puncture the black sky
above your house on a clear night.

Many more spin and twirl, gleam and flicker
their spikes in the space we call our universe.

Some folk say there are two hundred billion galaxies.
Others say the number is three trillion,
with as many stars in each one.

How much is a billion, a trillion?

A million seconds makes twelve days,
a billion seconds, thirty-two years.
A trillion seconds would be just under
thirty-two thousand years.

Two hundred billion galaxies
times four hundred billion stars,

makes for a lot of brilliance.

Doryn Herbst

Antinomian desert, wide open

torrid sun, a night's bite but no eyes
other than these, and no laws

other than these: no shout
or touch, no link or lattice

no interleaving of inside and out –
just calm here, experimental

in this wide open space that holds
solitary days and ways

before a quiet rush
to the world for some required hour

of sitting in a denser space
one person opposite one person

hard with no pretence, no drain
of goodwill, only transactions

of enough of the heartfelt
and more of the heartfelt

yet O'Keeffe, Beefheart, desert mothers
fathers and rats: the wide open space

already recalls its people
to the stretching horizon

of recovery – a re-covering where only fading
echoes of rush still sound

take up the brush
take up the pen

when sun dips below sand
when night scuttles inside a private heart

Pascal Fallas

Architecture of the Veil

mashrabiya

behind a latticed balcony
she sees faces, things passing,
early morning bread finely balanced

hears the call to prayer, humming
of ironmongers. Sikkat al-Badestan,
the lane of coppersmiths

beside blue shuttered doors
he etches a tray. Tendrils
of vines. A nightingale.

Marjory Woodfield

I Lit A Cigarette And Burnt A Hole In My Hand

That was just life under pre-Copernican skies
the spheres so near you could swing from them
held close in the ringing of the stars.

We'd balance ladders, lash scaffolding poles
a self-supporting framework in the windless air
but it began to sway as the children climbed.

There are no constants for every reference frame.
The cat in the box is alive but we outside
are both right and wrong about it at once.

Behind the gauze between the worlds
we own the worlds, at least we think
we might own what we think but

the fire roars, outside slow flakes of snow settle
we could never hold the horses of the tide
you open the book's cover and there's a hiss

release of something, not dust, some gas
some spirit fizzing into this close air
black ink that drinks the light, an infinite library

a different story for everyone that breaks
the back of your mind. Spark up from the fire
and I cup the cigarette in my palm

I burn a hole in this page and through it
see the stars shift on their greased axles
the cat among the cogs looking back at me

Geoff Sawers

Twilight

Sweat stains the couch. The body of a sleeping woman. Focus on her head. Focus on her eyes.

Look, blink, she is there.

Her back hunched. Her lips dried.
*
Offer a candle or a fruit. In front of the Virgin, ask for grace. Ask for protection.

She will answer, the fruit collects its seeds. Inside, the seeds peck the skin.
*
I repeat the word mother under my breath.

Focus on the pot stirring. Focus on the feet dancing. I follow the callouses of her heels. Clutch the edges of her dress.

She whispers child go to sleep.

Observe the sweat on her neck.
*
Beneath her hands, the uterus pulses. I gather what is needed: betadine, cross, needle.

The needle pushes in. We shift our focus to the sound of age: cracking bones, graying skin.

It is a candle on a cake that reminds us. I blow. The fire roars.

We run to the rooftops. I say tag. Mother runs. She runs and runs. Her legs, buckle and bend.

The north wind blows, pulling the body. Higher and higher! Her legs dance to the beat of the wind.

CJ House

Poem of Stars

In a dream I drink stars from a bowl like soup.
I drink stars until my eyes
   are nothing but starlight. In a dream

I burn my hands with stars. From deep in the forest,
I pray to night skies — altars of hazy light,
   sacred quiet light, and to the firestorm of a star's

terrible dream. I pray to a delirium of dying stars,
and at dawn, I wake into their ashes, into the memory
   of their fear, the miracle of their afterglow.

God's tiny poems are written with starfire,
and his bird-angel muse rises from Heaven's
   shadow, and flies joyfully

into a burning star. I see this from below
with my moon-mind, and I've learned Heaven's terrible
   love, the gift of suffering, and the mercy

of unbelievable heat — the open eye of a star,
and the patient mind of dark matter waiting
   for collapsing space of a black hole —

the way galaxies wait for their shred of love,
wait for one word of dying, one way
   to move into Heaven's dark-lit hush.

Alexander Etheridge

Misunderstanding

She thought it was his turn to cook and clean,
he thought it hers.

She counted him a fool, to vote the way he chose,
he only heard her say 'a fool'.

Let's wait and watch a while, he said. She nodded,
charging through the open doors.

He caught the words 'let's go', but when he turned
she hadn't moved, afraid to tread the path.

So many instances, so many years
familiarly misread.

They heed the health advice to stand apart
from others out in streets and shops and schools

by drifting far from one another's touch,
enclosed, alone behind their walls.

Like states whose cemeteries have space to fill,
they feel obliged to never end their wars.

Phil Vernon

How to Speak Love (Howe Sound, British Columbia)

in a snug two-seater heading cold-north
he needs his lover beside him
to have a sense of flow

the Sound vocal & coursing
alongside them

or perhaps it's that strapped to a leather seat
he can't stop his mind circling
what if...

he could just hear the two of them
streaming as tributaries one toward the other

but they're stuck
slow as road-melt
silent as lambent laden-cedars

frosted shut

how the trees sway how they glow
as one great blanket
falls to the ground

he thinks this is how it must be
to fade

without a sigh from a lover
or any sound
louder than breathing suspended

as a great grey owl hovers
in the sky

as his lover guides them
steadily forward
to a blinding storm of ice

Jeffery Sugarman

Between the bones

By the bed on your last day, I find
parts of you already gone:
spaces scooped between the bones

of your face and hands,
the unslaked skin of each soft dip
poised to slip should you stir,

like the hollow well
you taught me to make
in a bowl of sifted flour.

Karen Macfarlane

the space between our hearts

I like to think of space and time
as a ball of yarn, which means
the space between
you and me
is not infinite. It means
I could almost touch you—
all I need to do, is fold
the corners of the room,
wrap myself into the years.
What is space anyway? Who's to say
we're not still together? If
we could see things differently
maybe we could see there is
no space between us.

Simon Alderwick

A Personal View

Professor Al Filreis reflects on his experiences directing an open online poetry course on Modern & Contemporary American Poetry called *ModPo*, which has engaged 415,000 participants since 2012.[1]

Who keeps us safe?

It was exactly a decade ago, as I write this: I nervously clicked 'publish' on a 10-week online course about modern and contemporary U.S. poetry. Although the course was hardly new to me—I had offered it in classrooms since 1985 and had even taught it partly online and then entirely online since 1996 or so—the platform this time was robust and hot, all the media rage. I knew that the launch was likely to get a lot of attention worldwide. It did. The platform was relatively new, and some basic elements were not ready for prime time, quite creaky (the discussion forums in particular). But 2012 within weeks of my launch was going to be dubbed by the *New York Times* among others 'The Year of the MOOC,' and I pushed ahead despite the major unknowns. Heady moment. An open-enrolment introduction to artificial intelligence had enrolled 150,000 people. There were a few four- and five-week short courses on pop topics—on Time Management, on Writing Professional Emails, on 'A Life of Happiness and Fulfillment'— that enrolled 225,000 and more. How would modern—and indeed supposedly 'difficult' or, at any rate, *experimental*—poetry be received in the context of all this hullabaloo? I had no idea, but was game. And I stuck with my perhaps esoteric convictions about the not-easy art I admired. There would be no Robert Frost in the course.[2] And no confessional poets—no Lowell, no Plath. But there *would* be an incoherent, seemingly illegible New York Dadaist, Baroness Elsa von Freytag Loringhoven; a forgotten Depression-era communist (Ruth Lechlitner) who wrote about abortion; and an obscure Harlem Renaissance poet, Anne Spencer, whose poems about gardening had something to say about race.

The raging tech-world context for my ambitions as a teacher at that moment was, as my use of the infamous acronym above hints, the so-called *Massive Open Online Course*. It was free and open to anyone with a connection sufficient to stream low-bandwidth videos. My course would mostly entail reading poems on a screen of any size (outside the U.S. most participants typically would use phones or tablets), and then typing out

---

[1] https://modpo.org/
[2] Well, not quite true. There is one Frost poem in week 5 of the course, but it is presented negatively—a what-not-to-do instance in the context of modernism.

responses to what others were saying about the poems. We opened on September 4, 2012. That first season 42,000 people enrolled from 179 nations.

I was positively stunned by the response. The platform—provided by Coursera in its first season of offering a limited round of trial-basis courses hosted by a few universities—was built on the assumption that the lecture and quiz-taking would be the two main teaching modes. 'ModPo,' as we called our course, used neither; I as its founding teacher/convener felt that neither would make for an online course of much interest and, what's more, I had been harboring—and for years already had been writing about— a deep antagonism to such pedagogy. Our MOOC was meant, from the start, to be a course with real discussion at its centre. Read a poem. Then watch a video in which I led a collaborative close reading of that poem with eight colleagues—in which my role was to ask a few improvised questions and moderate enthusiastically so that all eight could take a turn responding to some phrase or line or word in the poem. *And then*, bolstered by the experience of seeing and hearing a close reading performed by a gathering of various minds and voices, go to the forums and post your own response, comment on others' responses, and try to figure out what the poem is saying in that community space. And that was it: read, watch others discuss, then yourself discuss, then repeat. Do that 119 times in ten weeks, in response to 119 poems, and you have an intensely interactive, often intimate, learning experience across time zones, generations, sensibilities, local educational attainment or social status.

Intimate? It is a word used again and again by participants across the years. Interviewed about her ModPo experience, early participant Tracy Sonafelt described the boisterous, structurally chaotic discussion forums: 'Sure, the forums can become unwieldy and [can] intimidate some because they are so huge...but eventually study groups and webs of connection with others of a similar mind make that vastness feel small and intimate and personal. If a student wants to be noticed, she will be; if she wants to hide, she can do that too. We are responsible for our own learning, and we are partners in shaping the 'curriculum' that is ModPo.' 'You remember how much joy there can be in learning,' observed Alice Allan from Australia. 'You'll see everyday things in a new light. ...You'll form new bonds with your classmates and become part of a community that feels both intimate and global.' Dorian Rolston, in an article about ModPo published in *The Paris Review*, pondered the MOOC in relation to its home base inside the 1854 Tudor-style cottage in Philadelphia called the Kelly Writers House. 'ModPo was designed to be the cottage's online extension,' Rolston writes, 'and it is, in some ways, just as welcoming.... [Filreis's] intimate pedagogy shapes the course site's very infrastructure.'[3]

Because I had already been teaching all-online courses, and because at my university I had long been advocating what in the 1990s was called 'teaching with technology,' I was familiar with a simple, persistent skeptical assumption: attempts to create a true learning community remotely, outside of the classroom with its traditions of spatial intimacy, would never replicate the human connection that is a prerequisite to education. From my involvement in various intra- and inter-campus initiatives—several of them during the techno-utopian moment of 1996-99—I had come to know the concerns of those who doubted the efficacy of such speculative focus, sudden administrative energy, and new investments. I was well versed in this distrust; indeed, in part because of the precipitous solution-obsessed attention by some university administrators, I had begun to share some of the doubts. How terribly superficial would the touted revolution be? Still, in 2012 I was not entirely surprised by the elated response of thousands of ModPo participants who were discovering each other as intellects and lovers of art despite the separations of distance and other social, economic, and linguistic factors of dislocation. Nor was I surprised by the affirmative responses of a few journalists who diligently covered ModPo in 2012 and 2013 as part of the 'Year of the MOOC' beat—those, I mean, who took the time to venture inside the community hosted by the course, talking with far-flung and exhilarated ModPo people. The key was not that a massive open online course could make college-level learning available and real to people anywhere; I still doubted *that* about the vast majority of MOOCs, in which you passively watched a lecture and took a quiz, and where the discussions forums were set up for the posting of questions seeking clarification of points made in the lecture or perhaps querying about deadlines or requirements, or seeking guidance in using the buggy, recalcitrant platform. But within several weeks of ModPo I knew that an open online course *need not be impersonal* if it could somehow invite learners to turn the platform toward the advantage of open discussion and interactive responsiveness.

What I did not expect was the particular political valence the MOOC would take on almost immediately. Some colleagues in the humanities felt that the quality of instruction in MOOCs was embarrassingly low, featuring simplistic mini-lectures in a format that left little to no opportunity for students to interact with the lecturer. While courses in several STEM fields and on vocational topics might perhaps succeed to teach skills and even concepts in this mode, the humanities, where iterative rounds of

---

[3] 'Free Verses,' Dorian Rolston, *The Paris Review*, December 10, 2012 (https://www.theparisreview.org/blog/2012/12/10/free-verses/).

interpretation were the key to learning, would be disadvantaged. (In contemplating this serious charge against MOOCs, we would have to ponder whether in large or even middle-sized in-person courses humanities professors have been successfully practising the sort of learner-centred interactivity found lacking in online instruction.) Others observed that 'Sage on Stage' academic superstars were being carelessly created, perhaps by opportunists, without much regard to real scholarly achievement in the fields they now far too widely represented to global publics forming their first impressions of U.S. academia. Still others resented the sudden euphoric attention of presidents and provosts while long-standing structural problems inside the university, directly affecting their own residential students, went unaddressed. Wild predictions were offered by columnists and national politicians about how MOOCs could radically reduce the cost of tuition, and about how much more 'efficient' this sort of teaching was or would become; these claims tended to alienate faculty further. (Dave Cormier in December 2011 saw MIT accrediting a MOOC for the first time and named it 'Black Swan 1' among his 2012 prognostications.[4] Thomas Friedman, in a widely cited column, declared that 'Revolution Hits the Universities' and that they would never be the same. Friedman quoted a 17-year-old with autism—Daniel Bergmann, who had taken ModPo and composed his first-ever essay—on Emily Dickinson's 'I Taste a Liquor Never Brewed'—in September 2012: 'I can't yet sit still in a classroom so [your course] was my first real course ever. During the course, I had to keep pace with the class, which is unheard-of in special ed.'[5])

Then there was the matter of which learners had first rights to all this knowledge and instruction now being given way, for free, to anyone. Here two academic leftisms converged or, rather, were being openly contradicted. One Left celebrated the liberation of paywalled academic knowledge, teaching and resources—a better fulfilment of the dream of many academics who had long decried ivy-tower barriers to entry, the sequestering of knowledge created at the universities (at significant public expense even at private institutions) to which ideally all people should have access. The other Left worried that the guild of hard-working and typically underpaid faculty was being undermined by university administrators and trustees seeking to score easy public and media points—and were betting they could soon enter wide 'new markets' of learners—by initially giving it all away *pro bono*. With this criticism there was some measure of felt solidarity with students whose families struggled to pay rising tuitions so as to gain hard-won access to resources and intellection now being freely

---

[4] http://davecormier.com/edblog/2011/12/19/top-ten-black-swans/
[5] https://www.nytimes.com/2013/01/27/opinion/sunday/friedman-revolution-hits-the-universities.html

appropriated and uncontrollably scattered, such that the precious costly degree might soon have less value.

I've tried here, in a short space, to summarise the complex first backlash against MOOCs—2012–13. A fascinating moment, to be sure. Elated as I was by the successful outreach through ModPo of the relatively little-known poetry I admired, I felt bitterly towards some of these rejoinders, mostly via Twitter disputes, negative reviews in higher-ed journals, and a few contentious on-campus conversations. Then I saw the backlash dissipate as soon as the headlines shifted from hyperventilating reports of radical utopian transformation in higher ed to dour accounts of MOOC drop-out rates and the struggles experienced by faculty seeking in the second wave to create their own MOOCs despite suddenly lessening incentives and rewards and institutional focus. ModPo continued to be free—a stubborn insistence of mine a decade later. Our essays were optional, ungraded, and peer reviewed. A small percentage of participants wrote and submitted them. Many people continued to be part of the ModPo scene, year to year, re-reading poems, getting involved with our 'SloPo' season (mid-November through August), signing up as Community TAs (CTAs), participating in our weekly live interactive webcasts during then annual Symposium Mode (September through mid-November), traveling to in-person meet-ups at cafes and bookstores around the world, setting up (more recently) weekly or monthly Zoom 'office hours,' and reading and discussing the scores of new poems being added to an augmentation of the main syllabus we call 'ModPoPLUS.'

I take the initial backlash to have been, ultimately, an expression of anti-utopianism. Critics of MOOCs did not give credence to chiliastic claims being made by or on behalf of deans and presidents and wildly growing for-profit groups such as Coursera or Udacity or Canvas Network. In taking such a view nearly all the sceptics missed how the radical ideals of the tiny, peripheral 'cMOOC' could be brought into the colossal, bulky 'x-MOOC' mode. People who were involved with 'cMOOCs,' the brilliant and chaotic Connectivist open online seminars, which preceded the star turn of the MOOC genre in 2012, continued to contribute important ideas about collaborative and hybrid pedagogies that influenced a few 'xMOOCs' (the cMOOCers' name for large, presumably impersonal, lecture-based MOOCs with their typically top-down, teacher-centered approach to learning). It was possible to see a future of xMOOCs, even those hosted by virtue of the backing of investors and through hastily arranged university/for-profit partnerships, that might benefit at least somewhat from the Connectivist vision of learners themselves learning how to alter the structures of learning; from participant-created workshop-style innovation; and from process-oriented rather than content-dependent collective instructorships. In that possibility one might discover, truly, that there is wisdom in a crowd. (I have written about this sort of enormous crowdsourcing as it applies to poetry, a field in which it is I believe especially apt—in an essay about ModPo called 'Citizen Poetics.'[6]) But again, though, the 2012-13 backlash was sceptical and dissenting rather than idealistic. I am less interested in that initial counterargument, and its internecine politics, than I am in the new wave of criticism that struck in 2020, when Coronavirus disease forcibly caused nearly all educators to teach online and the politics of online teaching became extensive.

This new backlash against online teaching was founded on a long-standing mistrust of centrist hopes and claims, and now was pitched against those who saw the moment as a chance to explore another 'silver lining' inside the severe social and intellectual restrictions imposed by the pandemic. The resistance came, distinctly to be sure, and variously, from both progressives and conservatives, from people who accepted the true health dangers caused by the virus and tolerated most mitigation strategies *and* people who could not abide any sort of top-down dicta. MOOCs already existed, of course, and were not a particular target of the new anger, which was directed generally at modes of remote instruction being hastily assembled at middle and upper schools primarily, and at colleges and universities. Few leaders in education at any level had had the sufficient resources set aside to make such a rapid shift and few teachers had had the experience, for instance, in leading a productive discussion using remote technologies.

ModPo had existed for eight years by then and had gathered around it a boisterous supportive community of current and former participants who, here and there, were now telling sceptical parents, teachers, family members, children and grandchildren about a massive online educational community that had been successful at maintaining itself and somehow encouraged intimacy as a prerequisite social trait of learning among others. Enrolments soared through the spring and summer of 2020, even though it was ModPo's annual off-season and in spite of my making no special effort to announce the year-round availability of the course. Many new enrollees told us they were there not for poetry but to see how the community constructed itself. The discussion forums began to fill with insightful meta-commentaries about which aspects of ModPo's collaborative approach could serve as models in response to the apparent dysfunction of so much online instruction (and workplace interaction) that nearly every family was experiencing. Much can be written—and will be, by me, when I have the time and page-space—about this erratic moment. And about the crucial differences between the backlashes of 2012–13 and 2020–21. And about

---

[6] Al Filreis, 'Citizen Poetics,' College English 47, 1 (Winter 2020), pp. 259-81.

why the sort of *poetry* presented in ModPo—open-ended and unresolved, supposedly difficult, requiring collaborative close reading—was and is especially pertinent to the crisis. Yes, I am certain that poetry has had something to say about all this.

'Crisis.' Of course we are talking about convergent plural *crises*, since many in 2020 began to face three urgent issues at once: the risky future of education, the effects of racist brutality, as well as of course the pandemic. Until I happened upon a speculative essay titled 'What Do College Students Think of Their Schools' Reopening Plans?' written by Masha Gessen for the July 11, 2020, issue of *The New Yorker*, I hadn't sufficiently appreciated how things had changed, nor how much the emergencies needed to be synthesised. Before contemplating that turn, we need to recall the early spring. NPR ran a story in which Anya Kamenetz coined the term 'Panic-gogy' to describe 'Teaching Online Classes During the Coronavirus Pandemic,' and the date of the piece is March 19. 'Online School Demands More of Teachers. Unions Are Pushing Back' is a *New York Times* headline of that moment. A far cry from Friedman's euphoria in 2012-13 over the coming new golden age of learning, Frank Bruni opined on June 4 in a column titled 'The End of College As We Knew It,' seeing restaurants and airlines as moving over the edge toward which higher education now also veered. 'Shakespeare gets kicked when he's down,' mused Bruni.[7] In the 'Recode' section of *Vox*: 'Paranoia about cheating is making online education terrible for everyone.' Jeffrey Young in *EdSurge* asked on March 25, 'Will COVID-19 Lead to Another MOOC Moment?' Rebecca Barrett-Fox outlined a new practical form of faculty resistance to administrators in a much-discussed blog post titled 'Please do a bad job of putting your courses online.' (Her opening line is 'I'm absolutely serious.')

Then, for many faculty, frustrations directed against the modes of remote instruction as they were hurriedly deployed in March, April, and May of 2020, gave way in the summer and early autumn to anger directed against administrators who by that point seemed much too eager to send everyone back into the classrooms for the new school year. The latter argument depended not on teachers' comfort or satisfaction with online teaching, nor upon the arguments in favor of the exploration of these astonishingly accessible pedagogies that could and perhaps should have been made by these same people in 2012-13. Which was now more despicable: remote teaching or educational leaders demanding that we quit remote teaching as soon as the exigent reason for it had begun to abate? The loaded institutional term for all this was of course 'reopening,' and Masha Gessen, investigating various easily ridiculed 'defense[s] of campus life in

---

[7] Frank Bruni, 'The End of College As We Knew It?' *New York Times*, June 4, 2020.

the pandemic' being now promulgated by colleges and universities, came upon the vital synthesis of social response to dysfunction that I realised only belatedly I had been seeking in the MOOC for a decade.

I will conclude here by summarising and endorsing the stunning point Gessen makes at the end of her *New Yorker* essay, adding assurances that I will explore it further in a longer study of learner-centred learning. Quoting a university president speaking sternly and with uncharacteristic conservatism about stern rules that would need to be imposed on students returning to campus while a pernicious disease was easily spreading (months prior to available vaccination, of course), Gessen observed the ideological irony of the authoritarian rhetoric: *'we have the authority to* put all kinds of expectations and requirements on our students' and to design 'a series of escalations for dealing with misbehavior.' Then, turning slightly toward an exactly contemporaneous situation, one involving many people of college age, Gessen described her research on the responsible and remarkably COVID-safe activities associated with mass anti-racist protests that had been happening in late spring and all summer in response to the murder of George Floyd in Minneapolis. Gessen, a veteran of protests (and long a journalist reporting on them), had never seen 'this level of detailed, organized, and consistent mutual care,' and quoted a call-and-response chant from the mass demonstrations—'Who keeps us safe? / We keep us safe!'— in such a way as to cause the renewal of antiracism activism, fears of the pandemic's effects, and frustration over the failures of 21st-century education to seem vitally convergent. Pivoting back to the situation of pandemic-era teaching and learning, she began tentatively to outline a learner-centred pedagogy, one that took its cue from people of the same age who made an effort to take the new politics into their own hands—a pedagogy that could begin with the 'community [that] students seek [pandemic or no pandemic] when they attend college in person.' She urged those in authority at schools to ask the students themselves, those *subject* (after all) to the old and suddenly outmoded (and, despite the shift to online, largely unchanged) methods of teaching, to create, as it were, a syllabus that included, rather than set aside, a fresh 'rethink[ing of] how colleges are interacting with students *who are staying home.*'

The people who have joined me for the ModPo experience, some of whom even admit to not liking poetry very much, are *ipso facto* 'staying home' for a variety of reasons, and the empathy Gessen briefly observed in young people during the summer of 2020 generally obtains. Just *one* reason for teaching ourselves to care about those who are staying home, since 2020, is obviously COVID-19. There are others, and they are relevant: no proximate access to a college or university; lifelong learning differences that made classroom learning impossible or at any rate disheartening and unproductive (witness Dan Bergmann); poverty in general and mass student debt in particular; overwhelming domestic responsibilities; chronic illness. Still another reason has to do with an emergent Connectivist sensibility, which, like the idea of the cMOOC still wandering in the wilderness, pushed even farther to the edges by the rush of 'Panic-gogy,' is what Gessen observed of learners realising their reasonable right to expect that the learning environments they enter, and indeed help create, will be built upon detailed, organised, consistent mutual care.

***

Al Filreis is Kelly Professor of English, Faculty Director of the Kelly Writers House, Director of the Center for Programs in Contemporary Writing, Co-Director of PennSound, Publisher of *Jacket2* magazine—all at the University of Pennsylvania, where he has been a member of the faculty since 1985. He has published many essays on modern and contemporary American poetry, on the literary history of the 1930s and 1950s, and on digital humanities pedagogy. Among his books are *1960: When Art and Literature Confronted the Memory of World War II and Remade the Modern* (2021), *The Difference Is Spreading: Fifty Contemporary Poets on Fifty Poems* (2022, with Anna Strong Safford), *Counter-Revolution of the Word: The Conservative Attack on Modern Poetry, 1945-1960* (2008). He produces and hosts a monthly podcast/radio program, 'PoemTalk', co-sponsored by the Poetry Foundation. He has won many teaching awards at Penn, was named Pennsylvania Professor of the Year in 2000 by the Carnegie Foundation and was named one of the Top Ten Tech Innovators in Higher Education for 2013 by the *Chronicle of Higher Education*.

The Interview

Caroline Bird is a poet, playwright and tutor. She has published six collections and recently a book of selected poems, won the Forward, been shortlisted for the TS Eliot prize and is interviewed here by **Mary Mulholland**

MM: I read that your first collection was published by Carcanet when you were just 15 and wonder if you came from a literary background? I gather your mother was a theatre director and your father an author. Did poetry feature much at home?

CB: My mum was the artistic director of West Yorkshire Playhouse – it was our unofficial babysitter as children. She'd be rehearsing, and we'd be wandering around, watching things that were definitely not age-appropriate! I had so much cultural privilege in terms of theatre, we had a house full of books. But the one thing my parents didn't read was poetry.

    The first poetry books I got were from Borders. I didn't know what good poetry was, so just picked good titles: *Trembling Hearts in the Bodies of Dogs*, by Selima Hill, still one of my favourite books, *Howl* by Allen Ginsberg, and *The Adoption Papers* by Jackie Kay. I'd been saving up to buy a portable television and blew all that money on poetry. I was about 12. I remember thinking 'Isn't this amazing. I'm not allowed to watch *Trainspotting*, but I can read *Howl*.'

    Poetry gave me access to this whole adult world that people weren't talking about to me, directly. I also liked the fact this was the one bit of art my parents didn't have a stake in. I'd write in secret, squeezed behind my bunk bed. I didn't really know what I was doing, but it felt truer than writing a diary.

MM: When did you start writing poetry?

CB: I was about eight. It was wildly precocious. One of my first poems was about a woman who could only exist in summer and a man who could only exist in winter who fell in love, but were doomed! I'd write about the most dramatic things I could think of. Then at 13 I won a Foyles Young Poet of the Year Award. The prize was to go to Lumb Bank[8] where I discovered this parallel universe: if you wrote poetry you were cool.

    Before that, at school, people would say I was 'a bit intense'. My 'best friend' found my notebook, shared it around and everyone laughed. It

---

[8] Arvon Centre

was horrendous. Then I won the FYP award and people weren't laughing anymore. I realised it didn't need to be something I hid. I was taught by Peter and Ann Samson, who encouraged me. Someone told me to buy *The Writer's Handbook*. I circled addresses. One was *PN Review*.

MM: Best to start at the top!

CB: I didn't know it was connected to a publishing house. I sent six poems, and got a letter back two to three weeks later, asking for all the stuff I'd ever written. I had about 100 poems, written when I was 13 and 14. In my memory everything happened very quickly. My book came out when I was 15.

MM: I notice the epigraph by James Tate at the start of *Rookie*. Has he been a particular influence?

CB: Tate and Hill were my first poetry loves, and later Sharon Olds. I remember getting James Tate's *Selected* when I was a teenager, reading the first line of 'I take back all my kisses': 'They got me because if the forest has no end I'll go naked' and that got me! I still can't tell you what it means, yet I also understand it. It makes me think of that Louise Glück quote, 'because it can never be entirely accounted for it can never be exhausted'.
      The James Tate quote at the beginning of *Rookie* is: 'Now when I address you/ it is somebody else speaking./ I couldn't be in two places at once, could I?/ *You sound like a real fruitcake, man.*'
      That's how it felt like putting *Selected* together. As if someone else was speaking or I could be in two places at once, because the poet I was at 14 was very different. I can hear echoes of me in some poems, some make me curl up and die, yet in some I was wiser, and there are poems that almost predict my life. It was an emotionally intense experience.

MM: Is there also something about whether a poem is an experience, an exploration, or perhaps both?

CB: There's a Marie Howe quote: 'the poem is an experience not the record of an experience', so even if you are writing about a memory the poem has to discover something you didn't know you knew in the process of writing.

MM: Do you have a checklist of processes to revise your poems?

CB: No, and every poem is a slightly different creature. I'll think pictures, I'll sense that this bit of the poem is a bit grey, or that bit of a poem is straining to find more, so might add a simile. It's very instinctual.

60

MM: How has your own poetic journey and editing process developed?

CB: As a teenager I wrote like I was on fire. I'd just sit down, full of pain and write. I felt very unheard. I knew I was gay at 13, had problems with bullying, and poetry was like picking up a phone to whoever I wanted to be. I loved being inside a poem, never got stressed whether it was good, because I wasn't writing it for anyone.

MM: So, poetry was safe?

CB: Yet dangerous, too, in a way that felt important. I was also entertaining myself and playing games.

What's interesting is that I'm trying to get back that same fire when I just wrote because I had to!

I would do a lot of editing later, but to begin with I'd step onto the blank page and just wonder. Now I still fling open the door of the first line to see what happens. My first drafts will be incredibly formless, unrecognisable to the end poem. The first draft is like hacking through vines in a jungle to make a path. With my second draft I return to the beginning of the path and go slower, taking in things I didn't see before. It might become longer, even more formless. 'Dive Bar' was a big block, and that whole thing about going into people's mouths didn't happen until a third through my first draft, when something had to happen.

By my third draft, I have created the spirit of this poem and need to find what kind of body it will inhabit. Say I've written a poem about a fevered love affair, I'll put that into a long column, with no full stops and line breaks in breathless places, like 'the' and 'it', because this poem can't control itself, and there'll be no stanza breaks right to the end. It makes sense with that spirit. Or sometimes you might think this poem has so much air and breath I'm going to create lots of white space and let it suspend.

In my first two books, and a bit of the third, I didn't work hard on shape. Republishing them, in *Rookie*, I've neatened them up, but didn't need to do much editing to content. These days I work hard at all stages.

MM: I find your poems supercharged, full of energy and surreal. Do you ever write 'quiet' poems? I'm thinking of the Tranströmer quote you use as epigraph in *The Air Year*.

CB: I find it hard to write poems without people, though the people might be fantastical. I write a lot of love poems. I don't think I've ever been able to sit down and write about 'a leaf'... I've always been freaked out by classical music. Not because I don't admire it but because it creates a stillness in my head that I find disconcerting. Part of what I love about poetry is how closely it links to dreams and one image slips into the next, and you know it's about your life, even if you can't pin it down. I think part of what I'm trying to do is create a dream while I'm awake, that is personal and true to me.

To be honest I don't have a huge amount of tranquillity in me. It's something I have to work quite hard at. I think my poetry is a reflection of my inner life.

MM: Might this connect to your playwriting, which is about people?

CB: Maybe. I didn't start writing plays until I was older. My plays are different in style to my poetry, but one thing I do think poetry and plays have in common is the dance of the unspoken. You can have three characters in a scene, and everyone is shouting, but somehow the truth is in the middle, not being said. In a poem it's similar, you can have a poem full of light and colour, noise and imagery and simultaneously it's not expressing the sadness at its heart. There is something quiet and true in the centre, wrapped up in the language of dreams.

Sometimes, people say my poems are quite funny, but whenever I look at them, I think 'god, that's sad'. Some of the funniest poems I've written have been when I am in most pain. A bit like standing on hot sand.

MM: This leads me to ask you about the role of obscurity and ambiguity in your poems...

CB: In *Rookie*, my most obscure book is *The Hat-Stand Union*. I had just come out of rehab, was very unwell and sad. It was almost like I had to obscure what I was writing as I was obscuring it from myself too. There's a poem called 'How the Wild Horse Stopped Me', which seems jokey, about a wild horse with a clipboard asking crazy questions, but it was actually a poem about depression and not being able to leave the house. Reading it, you probably can't tell. There's a quote by the psychoanalyst, Donald Winnicott, 'artists are driven by the tension between the desire to communicate and the desire to hide'.

MM: Did you write a lot when you were in rehab?

CB: There's a poem in *In These Days of Prohibition*, about how they took away my notebook. The first thing I did when I was given my 'Patient Intake Questionnaire' was to translate it into a surreal poem. I turned a line like, 'have you ever had a psychotic episode', into 'have you started looking at pigeons as if they know something'. I showed this to my counsellor who said I was using poetry to hide and they took my notebook away. There is an element of poetry that can be used as a refuge, to stay in that intense dream, as though it's about evading what is more painful: daily life.

At different points in my life I've tipped more towards hiding than communicating. Hiding makes you inventive, but in writing *In These Days of Prohibition* I made a semi-conscious choice to tip slightly back towards communicating, still using surrealism, but making my masks a bit thinner, letting the reader in more. I took that same feeling to *The Air Year*.

MM: Would you say you see poems like cinematography?

CB: I think more in terms of music and sound, imagery and colour, in terms of 'isness', and populating it, a sense that something's missing in the music. I want to feel it's all a game.

MM: What about your discipline of writing?

CB: With playwriting I am relatively 9-5, but with poetry I am still squeezed up behind that bunk bed, wanting to write whenever I can, even when I'm supposed to be writing invoices; I'll think 'Aha, now I'll work on my poem.'

MM: How important is the role of language to you?

CB: Really important. It creates the 'isness' in a poem. I love language. If you put a 'bucket' or thing into a poem, the abstracts take care of themselves. I think of language as populating the poem, making it more visible, but it's subtle too. I keep all my drafts, sometimes there'll be 30. But sometimes I go past the last draft: in getting a better word for this or that, suddenly it feels 'written' and loses its emotional intensity.

Often I'll be working to make it seem it's 'just written'. Some people ask if I edit my poems at all, and I'll be thinking I've just spent months on that! I try to make them feel like a stream coming down the mountain, rewriting to take away pebbles and make it run smooth. I've just finished a poem called 'The New People', for *Poetry Review*, which took three months. I had to keep rewriting it to let it roll down the page.

MM: Do, or did you belong to workshop groups, have mentors?

CB: I haven't had a mentor, never had a group – it sounds quite lonely! Obviously Michael Schmidt took me under his wing, but he let me just get on with it. But I've had mentees and that is like a duet of a process. I mentored Rachel Long and learned just as much from her. And I think it's important because poetry does get lonely. I don't generally send poems but

I sent Rachel a poem this week. I felt it wasn't finished, the ending was too neat, and she said, 'it feels like it's finished but it's not'. And I said, 'I knew it!' As if that gave me permission to find the real ending.

I teach workshops and especially love making up exercises. Recently I taught a masterclass about teaching poetry and writing exercises. Often what we need is to create prompts for ourselves. Sometimes I give myself exercises, such as, what would be the worst speech at my father's funeral? What if I wrote about what that pencil thinks of me. There is often a feeling that exercises are finite, but you can get multiple poems from the same exercise.

MM: And, generally, you don't run your poems past anyone?

CB: I read them to my partner. When someone knows you well, you can tell from their tone if something hasn't landed, so when she says, 'You've got it', I know I really have. Sometimes I show poems to my mum, that's about it.

MM: Do you write straight on a computer, or by hand?

CB: By hand, in my terrible handwriting! Very messy. Then I'll type it up, a shapeless block and work on it to see what it wants to become. I never want to prune the tree before it's time.

MM: And what poetic dreams remain unfulfilled?

CB: Every time I finish a book I feel I can't do this anymore. After *The Air Year* I had the longest period ever of not writing poetry. It started to scare me. Usually I'll have a period, maybe a year when ideas reform. Every time, I have to unlearn how to write a poem and relearn all over again, and I always want to try a slightly different thing. I'm more stable now. I used to wait until my life blew up and write from the debris, but now I have a toddler, a house, don't stay up till 3, so my next frontier is how to write from a place of dealing with the reality of life, rather than its drama.

MM: A bit like writing beyond the end of a poem.

CB: Exactly. My dream is for my next book to exist. I've written about six poems since my drought. I feel I'm learning how to do it with a slightly different version of myself.

MM: When you have droughts from poetry do you turn to writing plays?

CB: During my poetry drought I wrote *Red Ellen*, the life of Ellen Wilkinson. It was all-consuming. With playwriting I can write about emotion I've felt in the past. It's almost like acting. Whereas when I'm writing poetry, there's a plug socket to my heart, all the time. I wrote *The Air Year* in about seven months, I couldn't stop writing, it was quite painful and destabilising as a process. I think if I wrote poetry all the time, that would be a slightly dangerous place for me. Something about playwriting allows me to feel creatively expressed without the same intensity.

MM: I notice you're judging the Oxford Brookes Prize, what will you look for?

CB: A poem that as soon as I start reading I'm in it. We think poetry is about words ... but that's why poetry is impossible. We're trying to communicate something wordless using words. When you read a poem that really works, the words pass through your eyes yet enter your head so you can see and feel things, and it doesn't matter if you've read 300 poems that day, you're in it. It's that subtle mix of the music of language, the cinematography, the risk, the honesty. It can come in so many different forms. It's something where you genuinely feel 'aah': the line is connected, like a psychic phone call to someone else's interior life.

MM: Would you have some final words for our readers?

CB: Never be afraid of writing rubbish. You need a massive block of marble to make a sculpture, we all get paralysed by stepping out. The best place to start is with no idea where you are going: into the deep end, that mystery. The hardest thing is to fall and trust the net will appear. Once you've written your marvellous rubbish, you can start to sculpt, which is never as much rubbish as you fear it will be because it also contains your bravery.

Mary Mulholland

Caroline Bird's poetry published with Carcanet

Looking Through Letterboxes,
Trouble Came to the Turnip,
Watering Can, The Hat-Stand Union,
In These Days of Prohibition,
The Air Year, Rookie, selected poems

The Essay

Lesley Sharpe considers the element of space in 'The Glass Essay' by Anne Carson

'It is as if', says Anne Carson's narrator in the third section of *The Glass Essay*, 'we have all been lowered into an atmosphere of glass', where the French-Canadian context of Carson's writing also animates 'glass' as 'glace' – ice. Almost nothing can move. It is a space where 'Now and then a remark trails through the glass', but little of substance is shared. The words which do escape map out the minutiae of daily life and its intrusions: 'Taxes on the back lot', or 'Mice in the tea towel drawer again'. This scene of domestic confinement establishes for the poem the antithetical spaces of the mother's house and wide moor outside, where

> My mother's kitchen is dark and small but out the window
> there is the moor, paralyzed with ice.
> It extends as far as the eye can see

In another shift of reference, the poem also accumulates the resonances of Emily Brontë's domestic and imaginative life, set in a similar opposition, to create reflective surfaces and spaces by which Carson's narrator might also hope to arrive at some kind of clarity. *The Collected Works of Emily Brontë*, are, she says, her 'favourite work' ('THREE').

In its English sense, a 'glass' is used to magnify as well as reflect, and it is this shifting sense of scale, and therefore meaning, which concentrates so much of the energy of the poem. As lyric essay, it becomes a defining series of spaces in which Carson can develop an enquiry about self and love, about loss, absence and presence. The fourth section, 'WHACHER', also moves through the imaginative landscapes of the narrator's memory, to show space not only as the territories she inhabits, both large and small, but those intervals of time and distance which define her experience, subject always to reinterpretation. In an image which makes time and space synonymous, Carson shows Emily making 'her awkward way/ across days and years whose bareness appals her biographers', where this 'bareness', as blank space in the narrative, is shaped partly by her sister Charlotte's control, but also by the narrowing of the public space which Emily's consciousness is allowed to inhabit, for which 'the parlour' becomes the defining image.

Carson shows, however, that confining spaces not only freeze, but concentrate. By Charlotte's account, 'Emily is in the parlour brushing the carpet', and the biographers conclude that she spent 'most of the hours of her life brushing the carpet'. Thus, in Carson's intensifying repetition, this brushing of the carpet becomes an act of self-creation, cleaning as a polishing of surfaces, the tightly coiled energy of the scorpion 'crouched on the arm of the sofa' persisting as attendant daemon in the room. In another aspect, that potent energy meets its own image in the vast expanse of moor beyond the domestic territories, from which Emily, in the neighbour's account, returned 'with her face 'lit up by a divine light''. In Carson's poem it is the dimensions of lineation, of language and image, that are powerful enough to conjure 'moor wind and open night', undo 'the bars of time, which broke', and reveal 'the poor core of the world' which Emily 'whached [...] wide open'. Carson also shows, in pursuit of her narrator's own enquiry, that the contradictory imagery of Emily's poetry is defined by its tensions, its relationship with space,

> ...concerned with prisons,
> vaults, cages, bars, curbs, bits, bolts, fetters,
> locked windows, narrow frames, aching walls.

There is always for the biographer, however, a question: 'why all this beating of wings?' For Carson's narrator too 'there are many ways of being held prisoner', an awareness of 'the invisible cages that confine the heart and mind', and all are changeable. Where Emily can come in from her encounter with 'Thou', face shining, the narrator of Carson's poem finds in the expanse of moor a different kind of acuteness: the 'bare blue trees and bleached wooden sky of April/ carve into me with knives of light', all distance swallowed and closed, and a wind 'which now plunges towards me over the moor'. Time too opens and closes to create different spaces – there is 'the stalled time after lunch', claustrophobic, loud with the words the fathers 'never tell', and the year repeating 'its days [...] that other day running underneath this one/ like an old videotape'. There is the tight proximity of memory, of time, which 'still carries the sound of the telephone in that room' as if it were present.

Other energies persist to define spaces – there is the 'weather we may expect to experience/ when we enter Emily's electrical atmosphere', that space which will be, by her sister's account, 'a horror of great darkness'. For the narrator herself, 'There was no area of my mind// not appalled' by the submissive behaviour towards Law, the lover who has rejected her, which she watches in herself. However, watching also implies a shift of dimension, a space across which to observe or be seen, the 'whacher' who is both 'Thou' and 'thou', or the narrator herself looking down, in her state of erotic lucidity, on the objective bedroom scene below, bodies entwined there like Donne's lovers in 'The Exstasie'. These intertextualities create another space, where images and ideas reverberate to accumulate new meanings. The landscapes of the narrator's own experience merge with those of Brontë's fictional narrative and her biography, to develop a complex psychogeography,

> two souls clasped there on the bed
> with their mortal boundaries

> visible around them like lines on a map.

This is a different kind of nakedness to that of the first of the thirteen Nudes that will be developed in the later sections of the poem, but expresses a similar objectivity, where 'Nude #1. Woman alone on a hill', has only space and wind to define her, flay her, 'long flaps and shreds of flesh' ripped from her body. By contrast, between Charlotte's denial and the neighbour's account of Emily's 'shining' ecstasy, 'is a space where the little raw soul// slips through.' Carson brings to this image a powerful sense of poetic expansion in the image of that soul 'skimming the deep keel like a storm petrel,/ out of sight.' The complex image of the storm petrel energises the sense of release, symbolic of a person who brings or portends trouble, but also known to sailors as 'the gypsy of the waters', a colloquial derivation of a name for the Virgin Mary, and a divine warning of storms, or their cause. The alliteration in 'storm' and 'skimming', and the assonance of' 'deep' and 'keel' amplify the sense of length and breadth which counter both the narrowness of the containing space, and the opening 'space' through which the 'little raw soul' might make its escape, incorporeal, ephemeral.

The word 'space' here implies an infinite possibility, where an opening, even of a hair's breadth, might be something by which a being might enter or leave, be penetrated or released. The section 'WHACHER' becomes a pivot in Carson's lyric essay for the enquiry that comes before, and that which develops beyond it. The confinements of the domestic world recede as the portrayal of the thirteen 'Nudes', or visions, is brought to a resolution in the final one, Nude #13, which finds its corresponding spirit in the wide-open spaces beyond it. 'Nude #13 arrived when I was not watching for it', says the poet, in a closing of distance between subject and object; 'it was the body of us all' ('THOU').

Lesley Sharpe

The Reading

Watch the video

Pat Winslow reads and discusses her poems
'The Season of Burning Heather' and 'How Shall We Bury Our Dead'
which you will find on pages 24 – 25

The Alchemy Spoon
YouTube Channel

https://youtu.be/xoU-uB4ETt8

Reviews

Sue Wallace-Shaddad reviews a collection and two pamphlets that explore the complexity that makes us human, the world of Cornish mining and a poet's Sri Lankan heritage

Julia Webb
The Telling
Nine Arches Press, £9.99

Morag Smith
Spoil
Broken Sleep Books, £6.50

Sundra Lawrence
Warriors
Fly On The Wall Press, £6.99

Julia Webb's collection falls seamlessly into several parts. It unpacks the narrator's relationships with her mother, father, sister, grandparents, partner and son and introduces imagined daughters. The narrator establishes very quickly that she is not afraid of delving into the past and describing difficult emotional scenarios. This poet often uses extended metaphor as an approach to this challenge. In the first poem 'Crash Site', she writes of the 'wreckage of our mother'. The plane crash metaphor continues 'We never did find that black box' and the later line 'and each survivor told a different story.' Particularly hard-hitting lines are 'Our first memory was the screaming of metal/ and the silence which came after.'

Webb again employs metaphor in 'My father says he has forgotten how to make a storm'. This poignant poem, which describes her father as 'still the god of rainclouds', begins 'and though lightning still crackles from his fingertips/ he doesn't know how to throw it any more'. Webb captures a fractious domestic scene in the lines: 'he and our mother crashed against each other/ and made the most tremendous noise'. 'When I was made of concrete' explores the nature of a relationship through this unusual metaphor: 'I lay at your feet then – a path, a car park,/ waiting for someone to drive across me.' Concrete, however, does not start as a hard substance:

> and a sparrow alighted for a second or two
> mistaking me for something solid
> and left his tiny footprint on my skin.

In 'Birding', the subject of the poem is reimagined: '*Jenny Wren* he calls you on a good day'

> *morning chick*, he says,
> his fingers tangling in your nest of hair,
> it's then you offer him your song throat,
>
> and on a good day he can make you sing.

The narrator explores different identities. In 'The Hunt', the twists and turns of power in a relationship are represented through animal imagery. The narrator is, in turn, a bear, seal, lobster, bear again and then 'a marmalade cat' whereas the partner becomes 'a field mouse': 'When I had finished playing with you/ I crunched up your bones'. There is vivid imagery in 'That day I was a picnic rug', where the partner is a 'bottle of lemonade': 'Someone had shaken you a little too much./ I had a stain that wouldn't come off.' The narrator 'was a mermaid in 1974' in a moving poem about loss 'The future died inside me'. In 'Women as collateral damage', the poet muses upon the behaviour expected of women. The lines 'I was cloudburst as a child/ never a pink fluffy jumper' encapsulate the child's character.

'Selves (non existent)' is a clever list poem using the anaphora 'self' at the beginning of each line. The poem presents photographic images, such as, 'Self at top of Eiffel Tower', but some are surreal as in 'Self as snorkel'. The ending is unsettling:

> Self protesting up a tree
> Self at end of rope
> Self exploding like the sun

The word 'Because' starts each couplet in 'Jewel Thief'. The poem ends on a worrying note: 'Because in your new suit you fitted right in/ and no one was the least bit suspicious.' This anaphora is also used effectively in a poem about the narrator's relationship with her sister 'Ten Excuses for Not Phoning':

> Because there is stuff hidden in your attic.
>
> Because of the lies we told and the lies we tell ourselves.
>
> Because of those games we used to play.

In 'Escape' the repetition of 'I didn't' at the beginning of several lines builds a sense of guilt in the self-awareness portrayed, in the avoidance of confronting a situation. The poem ends: 'I let you be the one to do the leaving/ so that I could be the one to cry'.

Prose poems punctuate the collection, sometimes with the use of slashes in the text. In 'girl was born' this creates a sense of dislocation. As elsewhere in the collection, the subject takes on other identities: 'girl was a ratty tennis ball/ somewhere along the way she lost her bounce'. The prose poem 'Grandma' turns rather sinister: 'her fairytale traps/ her witches brew/ her head on fire/ her house on the hill/ her trail through the forest/ her hidden knowledge/ her basket of lies'. 'Fuck Body' (after Inua Ellams) has pithy phrases: '/ colossal pit of want/ the place where magic's supposed to happen/ perhaps it did once'.

The poems, though often dark and even surreal, are not without humour. In 'Your sister is blaming you for the rain' the narrator describes her sister cutting contact, 'the note says *it's for your own good*' but is then faced with her sister turning up at a poetry reading 'with her buzzard and a pint of Diet Coke':

> The big decision now, you decide,
> is whether to stick to your planned reading
> or break out the Sister poems.

'My glasses say' is an inventive poem which ends: 'We have a co-dependent relationship – they need me so they can see the world'.

There is such an emotional range in this collection. 'Giving Thanks' is a touching poem about the narrator's son 'I am trying to coax my grown-up son/ out of the smog of his own thinking.' The poem 'You see love as a bonus' analyses love in powerful contrasting couplets:

> You see love as a hot slap
> of a palm against the cheek
>
> whereas I see love as a rogue planet
> fast moving and mysterious

'A perfect square of blue' is a gently nuanced poem about the reaction to hearing bad news: 'I can't remember now but I imagine that bread was burnt'. Webb's poetic skills and her raw honesty shine throughout this compelling collection.

'Sky Disk', the opening poem in Morag Smith's pamphlet, describes 'the Island of Tin', a moniker which aptly sums up the way Cornwall, with its mineral riches, once seemed unique and remote. Smith's poems are grounded in the ancient physicality of the landscape. She pictures a seam of tin as: '300 million/ years lying like a blanket over its bed of rock'. A cliff is described in 'Prima Materia' as 'folded by birth/ like an impossible mattress'.

The poem 'Heligan' builds up a powerful aural and visual representation of memories of this land. The repetition of 'found' instils a drumbeat throughout the poem and echoes the first few lines:

> This dark place
> is mud-bound
> Underground
> Sub-stratum
> of a sub culture

There is beauty to be found in this landscape. 'Ictis' describes 'the moon people/ forging ancient island tin':

> Mark the angle between the blue-green patina
> and an inlaid rainbow
> melt the metal crescent and the stars

The particular language of mining and miners proliferates in this pamphlet, creating a sense of otherness: 'vanning', 'spalled', 'bucking iron', 'kibble', 'cobbing', 'genny' and 'slag'. The word 'spoil', which gives the pamphlet its title, also recurs. Cornwall is marked by its mining history and this word encompasses a sense of what is left behind. In 'Great Flat Lode',

> Spoil
> rising gently to the lip
> once heaped up
> now falls stone by stone

This is poetry that is not just about the land, but very much about the people who mined the tin and branches into the modern-day experience of the itinerant worker. The four poems which make up the 'Bal Maiden' sequence present a hard-hitting picture of the young women who break up the rock. The fourth poem 'Copper Mine' describes the levels of strength needed by men but also by small children. Using a barrow, 'a pair of girls' have to push 'a half/ hundred weight between them'. The second poem 'The Bal Maiden Breathes Out' is in the voice of one young girl. Speaking about the mine, she says she is

> breaking her up
> smashing her face
> like I ain't felt the fist
> like I don't know she hurts

The third poem in the sequence, 'Eliza Allen – Truro, March 10th, 1841', is particularly striking in its portrayal of the harsh realities of a female miner's existence. Eliza has 'feet wet' and 'breathing problems', so much so

> that she don't sing
> with the other women
> as they open up the stone

Interspersed through the pamphlet are modern-day poems about life on the road. In 'Elvis the Enforcer',

> We drive from farm to farm
> awaiting a harvest
> that never comes

We learn of the symbiotic relationship with the official who must move on the travelling workers. He writes 'empty threats' but also 'takes tea by the fire'. In the poem 'Rabbits', a neighbour says, 'we're queens of the road'. The poem goes on to detail skinning a rabbit with the help of four-year-old daughter Betty, delicately describing a moment that is both harsh and tender:

> Betty hefts the little axe
> but misses
> cuts its ear in two

There is a strong sense of threat in 'Leaving' where the workers face 'being burnt out' if they don't move on within the week:

> the enemy he made
> came today
> like a snarling dog
> meanly slinking round

74

The threat becomes reality in 'Cold Night' when their car is 'torched'. The poem, 'Eye on the Mirror', captures anxious moments when starting to drive away 'ten tons of truck', but once on the road 'I want to drive to / the edge of the land.' The driver is also 'waiting for the inevitable / blue light'. It is clearly a life of peril but there is also pleasure; in 'Cold Night', 'muffled laughter escapes thin aluminium walls'. These poems also convey a warm sense of community as the narrator says she can:

> watch my neighbour's windows
> looking for familiar silhouettes
> their trailers white in the small light of distant stars

This pamphlet brings to life different aspects of Cornish life and landscape in dramatic and engaging ways. The language is sparse and to the point, often written in short lines. The final stanza in 'Fire in the Hole' is particularly evocative of the passing of time:

> Mines are empty churches
> The silent bell tower
> no longer smokes

***

Sundra Lawrence evokes the complexity and richness of her Sri Lankan background in her debut pamphlet. The opening poem, 'Rasam' introduces us to fiery Tamil food with the mention of Icarus implying the heat of the sun: 'Icarus pepper, garam masala,/ flesh-soaked tamarind'. Heat also features in the picnic scene described in 'Somewhere in Normandy': 'we pick at *sambal* so hot it breaks plastic'. This poem also celebrates dancing, 'metronome feet wake dirt, /lost in *Baila's six-eighth* beat'. Its last line states 'Cut the island and it will bleed music.'

The pamphlet's title comes from 'Warriors', an ekphrastic poem which is both lyrical and hard hitting: 'We never asked to be made like this,/ brutal and injured totems.' 'Jaffna', written in two parts, 'I. 1989' and 'II. 1991', charts the collapse of Lawrence's mother's house in a bombing attack and the mother leaving Jaffna with her two children on hearing of her father's death:

> Under a sky of pawned gold,
> you three arrive at your mother's door—
> your father already hours in the ground.

In 'Summer '95', the family are stopped by a police officer but when he learns where the poet's mother grew up,

> *Mutawal*. He repeats, his mouth relaxes
> on each syllable. *That's where I'm from.* His voice
> is song, neighbourhood song and when did she leave?

The library in 'The Jaffna Public Library of lost books', represents 'The lungs of Tamil culture'. The reader learns of '100,000 books burnt to black pollen'. Religion and belief come into question in the sequence 'Flame'. There is a particularly striking line 'I pretended to be a pew, my bone pinned to the beam' in '1. Holy Communion'.

'Honeymoon, South Goa' has a striking image: 'A teaspoon of sunlight opens the dawn' and the pamphlet ends on a very lyrical note in 'Grown Up',

> bathe in a sky blown clean;
> let the land purr with full cups
> of sun and washed plates.

Lawrence's poems span childhood, adulthood, the challenges of culture and identity, giving the reader a tantalising insight into her heritage.

Sue Wallace-Shaddad

Lesley Sharpe considers the uses of power in poems that address poetic, political and religious authority

Michelle Penn
Paper Crusades
Arachne Press, £9.99

Naush Sabah
Litanies
Guillemot Press, £8.00

In poems that are as inventive in their forms as in their language, Michelle Penn's sequence *Paper Crusade* explores the many uses of power. Inspired in part by an interpretation in dance of *The Tempest*, Penn's poems draw on and move beyond the intertextual reverberations of Shakespeare's play to unfold themselves in voices that are both archetypal and unpredictable, reaching deep into imaginative territories that can also shift their mould – the sea and elements, the nameless father, brother, girl and boy, the spirit and indigenous character of 'C'. The place of nature, patriarchy, master and servant, authority and authorship – all will be redefined, and the conceit of paper as mask, as book, will open into a drama where paper itself becomes the materiality of both text and performance. The hermetic book of 'The Father' will ultimately be reclaimed by the sea, and his attitude of mastery deemed by it, even at the opening of the sequence, to be 'an impertinence', for '~ No one games/ the sea ~' ('The Sea, offended'). Penn also ensures that there will be revisions of the colonial appropriations and impositions of language, where, in an early poem, 'C faces the morning's burdens', the unnamed C can observe that he is also

> / the h-horse / / of your best / / intentions /
> /s-saddled with your words/ /you t-taught me
> glass// but I knew lightning

These mercurial shifts of language are possible in a world where glass is also mirror and shard, the hard glinting sand, the cutting 'rain' that disfigures the girl, leaving her both 'ravaged' and 'ravishing' – a characteristic play of language in which Penn dismantles and reverses expectation to create the sudden electricity of an unexpected image. The girl, though damaged, is now a heroine in her own right, even with

> ~ a face
> shattered ~ in a rain
> of glass ~

but The Father will retain her in his imagination as 'a gem/ formed in the pocket of my intellect'. The relics and images of the civilised world glint and shine with their own brightness in these poems – 'black leathers strangely pristine', 'night silks flaring', a 'tiara' of blond hair – and in 'The Sea watches The Father at his favourite game', the magic 'tomes' of the Father, though 'crusted with salt and sand', are still alive with this kind of lexical potency:

> This one ~
>   sapphires spilling from pages ~
> That one ~
> emeralds ~ diamonds ~ pearls

For all its apparent brightness, Penn shows the darkness of a power that would make a slave of air, of music, of the natural. She delineates the ways in which this power jangles against a life at home in the elemental world – that other power, other magic, with its own language, unformed, always forming. The girl too, in 'The Daughter considers the status of monsters', recognises that C

> does not frighten me
>   ...i remember us... diving the black
>   shallows... stabbing
>   barehanded and blind... for fish...

Through imaginative experiments in form and punctuation, space and silence, line and stanza break, Penn creates a drama which shifts the central focus from a Prospero-like character, and the attendant questions of justice and redemption, to encompass a consideration of the elements themselves. Moving on from the moral landscapes and brave new worlds of its intertextual histories, her story arrives in the political and ecological landscape of our own moment, 'the sun/ firing high, not even a shadow to shelter beside' (The Boy awakens). The enduring backdrop is one of remorseless heat, the sun 'vicious', 'flagrant', with a pervasive scorch of burning sand, 'sun, sun, and sun', and 'the searing light'.

Penn's 'island of perpetual sun' of the opening poem resonates throughout the sequence, with its suited paper crusaders in 'banker-suits, gloves, paper masks' ready to fulfil the high rhetoric of the 'quest for revenge', the crusading spirit of The Father. With the righteous call to arms, his is an imperialism redeemed always to itself by the idea of salvation. But what will be saved? For what? Or whom? From what or whom? The Father imagines a return to his 'empire across the sea', as if the long arm of space delineated in the words 'empire' and 'across' could conjure old certainties of authority, but he disregards the sea itself, always a dominant voice in the sequence, and an undercurrent which Penn weaves through the other voices: '(the waves)/ [...] (the words)'.

These are poems in which words move with the independence of waves and dreams to interrogate what can be governed and by whom, in a world where 'history only bows to revenge'. Penn's blank paper masks conjure that ancient sense of theatre, anonymous, essential, which invites opposing archetypes of comedy and tragedy to pull against each other. Will the lovers find happiness? Will the hubris of the wicked brother bring his fall? Will there be forgiveness, reconciliation, an end? As 'proud leader, Father/ to you all', the patriarch has appointed to himself an unnatural power, 'spells only a god/should throw', so that this can never be the end. As the Japanese proverb has it, 'even the reverse has a reverse', and in this sequence, both lyrical and dramatic, Penn ensures that the expectations are constantly shifting. Nothing is reliable, or without consequence. It is not enough to be

> suited...masked...
> as though intentions unseen...
> ...simply cease...
> ('The Daughter considers the status of monsters')

'*The Tempest*', said Victor Hugo, 'is the supreme denouement, dreamed by Shakespeare, for the bloody drama of Genesis. It is the expiation of the primordial crime.' Shakespeare's story has its twelve-year delay, the hoped-for anagnorisis, the very real possibility of a brave new world. *Paper Crusade* gathers its own ecological and political momentum through the force of poetic innovation. In a world ravaged by heat, where water moves with its own primal power, the ecological as well as the post-colonial consequences reverberate, inseparable, no less powerfully than a primordial crime. Penn skilfully reframes the drama, the questions, the voices and their authority. Rhetoric and lyric give way to silence, and even paper cannot be said to have the last word.

***

Naush Sabah's debut pamphlet *Litanies* opens with a compelling account of the narrator's renunciation of religious faith, her Islamic inheritance and its authority. 'I dared', she says,

> – and made eternal life
> blur into oblivion
> taking my fears with it

Faced now 'with fathomless black/ and no promises', Sabah's narrator articulates the challenges and shifting moods of her decision, the slow or sudden falling away of belief, and the long reverberation of its authority, where 'disbelief is the heaviest element/ with the longest half-life' ('Litany of Desolation'). Enduring the silence of God, the deceptions of self and family, the 'remorse/ I can no longer muster', the narrator finds that religious monuments, too, have become a kind of shell, another long echo, where 'the deities have died but these columns endure' ('Of Monuments'). What has been lost is a world where 'words bounced off her before causing doubt' ('Of Yaqeen'), where *yaqeen* is certainty.

Ultimately it is words which shape and expand Sabah's enquiry. Inventive and varied in their forms, her poems address litanies as a series of petitions to the absolute authority of the divine, but also as a series of increasingly meaningless repetitions of language and form, repetitions designed to shape the day, the whole life. The word 'litany' itself, with its Greek root in the idea of supplication, conjures a sense of prayer and appeal that runs strongly through the sequence. In the 'Litany of Desolation' the narrator recognises herself as the 'seeker', the 'supplicant' who

> has asked for openings,
>   asked for unveiling,
>   for noor to descend.

Sabah shows that these are words and practices woven deep into the narrator's very being, 'the oft-repeated verses', where God is the 'longed-for salvation', and the answering silence the 'saddest story', the 'cruellest trick'. In the accomplished poem 'Mercy', she uses the specular form to expose the flexibility of language, aligned here to the north star of faith and religious authority to achieve the needed answer whatever the circumstance. Again, in the masterful 'Sestina for Salah', she dramatizes this process of alignment from birth: 'Before Bebo can speak or stand/ the call to prayer is raised'. As the child becomes mother, she too 'commits and bows', but it is the sestina form itself that allows language to make the journey to a new possibility, where, in the final stanza, her own daughter, who now 'prostrates and kneels', leads Bebo to ask if she 'might stand, might rise'.

In other moments confinement gives way to exhilaration, as in 'Litany of the Shoreline', where Sabah addresses the problematic consciousness of seeing and being seen. In this examination of nakedness and the veil, she explores the highly cultivated 'art of looking away' to work free of prohibitions which, imbibed from birth, have become inhibitions. The narrator's headscarf billows at first 'white as surf', 'a curtain/ or a flag', but then, in a sudden and sinister shift of language, is 'hanging like/ a noose a mask'. Expanding beyond the internalised authorities which watch her, the poem with its fluid form expresses a transformation of the narrator's consciousness, moving through the sensuality of air, its touch, 'the kiss of breeze', to the shoreline

> still shining
> gold bare
> bare

and the rising energy of a body 'running by the shoreline', moving always towards a new imaginative possibility where even 'the eye of the land is looking at me', and 'no veil covers me'.

This legacy of concealment is explored in poems about coming of age as a young woman within the patriarchal structure of Islamic faith, with its attendant taboos around sexuality. In 'Questions of Faith' the narrator expresses frustration with its apparent double standards and flaws of logic, where 'there is no end to things Muslim men can be/ forgiven at home & punished for outside', while elsewhere she notes that 'hell is filled with bad women' ('Litany of Dissolution'). In 'Creation Story' she portrays the young women who resist their tradition, 'arriving in the cars of boys we don't know', visibly embracing the very thing that is feared in a kind of extravagant exhibitionism:

> See them spread across the country and world
> in search of sex and freedom.

Sabah's language is also spare and shocking to enumerate the cost for girls who must 'marry in secret and abort the contents of their wombs', and the dramatic tension at the heart of lost faith is not only fuelled by the question of salvation, but the loss of cultural meaning and community, its coherence. 'I'd been anchored,' says the narrator, 'saved by certainties' ('Lament to the Lost Door'). Early in the sequence, 'Litany of the Lake' establishes the original dislocation, which drives the weight and force of history to a new geography. Its 'old authorities' are tenacious, surviving with their power to bestow, to withdraw, to honour, 'to raise and hew' in a new environment, where in the opening 'Litany of Dissolution' the supplicant can still implore:

> some father   forgive me
>   some shayk   some patriarch

However, the formal space here creates silence, and ultimately the poet's enquiry returns to the question of how an individual might find her own words, her own meaning, explore what can and can't be done, what can and can't be spoken, forgiven, for whom and with whom. This is a brave volume which explores the tensions encountered in the search for self-determination, culminating in the narrator's complex realisation that

> God always spoke
> in the tongue
>   of other people,
>   needed me to be
>   someone other than me.
>
> ('Litany of Desolation')

Lesley Sharpe

Diana Cant finds her superficial sense of a half-familiar world becomes gradually unsettled

Jo Clement
Outlandish
Bloodaxe Books, £10.99

Jo Clement is a lecturer in Creative Writing at Northumbria University, and editor of *Butcher's Dog* poetry magazine. She has also edited *Wagtail: The Roma Women's Poetry Anthology* (Butcher's Dog, 2021), and has published two pamphlets. This is her first full collection.

These poems address her heritage, and the Gypsy, Roma and Traveller culture in a rich, lyrical and beguiling way. But they do rather more than that: they convey the sense of being an outsider, yet it is we, the readers, who are the outsiders. We know some of the cultural language, it resonates with us, often in a half-formed, half-known way, so that we are confronted with a world that is partly familiar, yet not properly grasped. Increasingly, we realise that there are levels of meaning that, as 'gorgers' (non-Travellers), we do not understand. But we are offered a window through which to see this world, from the outside, looking in. Clement does this with particular skill; she does not alienate her readers with polemics but carries us with her in our desire to know more. In addition to the poems there are footnotes and end-notes – these, as well as being illuminating, also serve to highlight that there are further layers of meaning to be uncovered if we wish to reach a deeper understanding of the culture.

The poet has said that Gypsy, Roma and Traveller people are 'everywhere and nowhere', and the title itself *Outlandish* signposts the idea of 'out' versus 'in', and the importance of land or no land. Such dichotomies often characterise this collection – the poems offer a glimpse of an inside world whilst relaying a sense of the outsider; they look both forward and back, they are ancient and modern, they are settled and unsettled; they are restless, they describe 'the skim of blood that cannot settle'.

Clement often writes in couplets, with a finely-tuned musical ear and much internal rhyme. She chooses images that are rich in associations and which conjure a vivid soundscape – for example, from 'Family Silver':

> Let me sing of my greatest
> grandfather's knife. He graved
>
> the tooth with scrimshaw cobs,
> so he might remember to handle

the blade as gently as his horses.
Kept it sharp enough to gut a trout,

split a clutch of pegs. Sharper
still to cross palms with silver,

In four couplets we are given five cultural signifiers, and although we may think we recognise this world, as the collection proceeds, we become aware our knowledge is superficial. There is an economy to her descriptions. 'King Faa' takes some Romani words to describe a mercurial, moonlit world, whilst drawing on authentic Gypsy history:

No patrin, no shock
of grass, his moonlit flit

brings farness. No kettleflute
til Christmas,

no fiddlescrape,
or bow-top brake…

tin pinched tight
as coney skin.

and we are left with a sense of strangeness, another world existing in parallel with our own. There are descriptions of the natural world that are both familiar and unearthly – 'pressing as a lurcher kneels onto a hare' ('At Eidon'); '(she) urges a nightjar to chirr/ his haggle's shape' ('King Faa').

Some of the most effective poems are those that juxtapose the old ways with new cultural and societal shifts. Sometimes this occurs within one poem, sometimes through the thoughtful ordering of the collection. In 'Vault', the new generation of settled Traveller girls ride:

leaning gravestones
like ponies

their mouths stuck
with brambling

nettle-stung ankles
grazed giddiup green.

A girl waits for a boy 'listening for his quad's buzz/ up and down/ the Queen's highway', ('Teesdale Erratics') – a scene referenced later in a description of the sulkie races at Appleby Fair on 'the mad gypsy mile'. 'The Graver' combines an archaeological image with Ladies Day at Ascot, building on words with double meanings:

> a stirrup
> from the Steppe,
>
> moored so long ago
> it turned lyre string,…
>
> Ladies Day fox furs
> and fascinators,
> screwed up slips.
> Greed as long
>
> in the tooth
> as grave goods
> or steeple-high
> hawthorn.

and also encompasses a painting by George Stubbs. So much ground is covered, with so little seeming effort. A modern-day rag-and-bone woman gathers white goods rather than rags, and Traveller girls shy away from a photographer's exhortations during a Stella McCartney advertising shoot – 'pinch petunias/ from pub planters/ push stalks behind ears' ('Market').

The word 'settle' evokes powerful associations in these poems – a traveller dilemma never truly resolved, we come to understand. A woman, having been excluded from church for 'not dressing right', walks her baby in his Silver Cross pram – 'she knows he'll not settle' ('Mass'). Pollarding apple trees is used as a metaphor for settling ('Pollard'):

> her freckled hands
> in the window lifting nets
>
> to arrange polished porcelain
> to say we are horse people.
>
> We've settled.

And even, in 'Tinker's Tea',

> The Settle line brought me to these hills.
> Maned in winter, he makes tea the old way.

If there is a unifying beat to this collection, it is the ever-present thrum of horses' hooves. We are made keenly aware of the centrality of the horse – or 'hoss' – in Romani, traveller and Gypsy life. Horses become a constant in a perpetually shifting world; they move in and out of many of these poems, and whether their presence is solid flesh, or something more ancestral, they always carry culture and tradition on their back. In 'Singing Lesson', a conventional, and unsuccessful, riding lesson is set against one given by a grandfather:

> The lass slapped me in a helmet, clipped me
> to the bridle, had me rising up and down,
> fairground pink and prim...
>
>   When Grandad came back...
>   Had me up on a muddy cob
> slow enough not to spook the traffic,
>   down the road where they zipped
> sulkies through red lights.

There are more references to Appleby Fair, the iconic annual gathering, where horses are displayed and traded on the banks of the aptly-named River Eden, and are washed with:

>   lines of Fairy Liquid, luminous and slick,
> drawn along each piebald's spine.
>
> Grease lifts. First withers then river turn to bubbles...
> We're immersed in this baptismal Eden.

and in 'Flash', we're given a vivid piece of the action – 'these lads/ zipping by on sulkies stood in a bevelled blur/ of bare chests, hooves and Brylcream'.

Finally, 'Self-portrait as 100 Travellers' is a forceful break from the poet's preferred couplet form. It is a blocked prose-poem, comprising a list of names used for Travelling people, starting with 'Here', ending with 'Gone', and with 'Me' in the middle of the work. It is perhaps the most powerful of the poems, and Clement has said that it was the hardest to write.

This is a collection that repays rereading, partly for the musicality, partly for the vivid, economical imagery, and, importantly, for the window that it opens on a culture that many of we 'gorgers' think we know about but, in reality, understand very little. The final lines prove an apt summation, perhaps echoing The Tempest, referencing both ancestry and endurance:

We of the black curl
bear these tides.
We swallow pearls.
We swallow time.

Diana Cant

Mary Mulholland reads bewitching poems exploring neurodivergence and female love

Jane Burn
Be Feared
Nine Arches Press, £9.99

As neuro-divergence becomes more commonly discussed and acknowledged, late diagnosis can help some people make sense of their life. This is Jane Burn's experience and the poems in her debut collection explore this through a richly imaginative blend of fairytale and fact.

Jane Burn is also an artist and her striking painting on the front cover prepares us for poems that incorporate spiritual, mythic, folkloric and feminine perspectives. Reading the titles would be enough to convince any reader that this is going to be a richly rewarding read: 'Thumbelina's Birth as Told in the Style of Gregorian chant'; 'Gerda's searching leads her to roses and, at the edge of the Snow Queen's land. she realises that her Autism will always be the fairytale with no satisfactory end'; 'Aubade to the Noise of Chainsaws'.

The title is from her artwork on the cover, but several poems contain the imperative 'Be'. In 'Be subtle as the Snow Queen' she urges us to 'Be giddy on goat-shaped legs'; 'Be the catastrophe of mountains.' In 'The gifts she got at birth': 'Be beautiful'; and the collection title comes from the poem 'This is a Frankenstein Night' with its exhortation to 'Rebuild the monsters in your life' and 'Be feared that someone might grab your back, pull out your lungs, crack your spine'. Definitions of fear include reverential awe, frighten, be afraid, and this title suggests the sense of empowerment that comes from confronting fear.

The collection opens with a poem alarmingly entitled 'Trepanation', an ancient surgical intervention of drilling a hole in the skull, whereby the poet finds 'I opened my head to the luminous fusion of stars' and 'uncovered a world' which seemed to liberate her and 'I could not taste the ghosts that I had kept'. In 'The Only Kind of Poetry I Seem to be Able to Write' she writes, 'I prayed to be/ the perfect mum and if not that, allow my love to be/ a natural thing'.

Many poems are in the form of a prayer or litany, even if ironically. In 'Mrs/Mother   Hail' Burn writes: 'Mrs/Mother   blessed are the windowpanes/ O keep us from the lure of dust'. The poet seems to be questioning her own faith in several poems referencing church, especially Catholicism, as in 'Look at me, lingering outside this murdered church' where she exhorts 'If I am to believe, daub me some vivid grief/ gouge this wasted cave with a burning of Sacred Hearts'.

Another issue close to the narrator's heart seems to suggest lost love, as in 'So you made a thousand shit decisions': 'When you felt him in you   you cried   when you kicked your legs/ it was too late and you he said   had been   *broken in*'.

The poet has a wide and very wonderful lexicon, so, in 'Aubade to a Wedding Photograph', 'the creep of early sun/ knifes the curtain's gap' when the poet will 'leave you in the shipwreck of our bed. Slipper/ the cold fish of my feet', creating an almost mythic quality. In other poems Burn subversively reworks Rapunzel, Snow White, Alice in Wonderland and others.

In the heart of the book is 'Frances Cornford's poem about a lady in gloves makes me realise that I have feelings for a woman for the first time'. Here the speaker muses on her own 'indelicacy' 'studded with magpie brooches,/ big feet primly tucked. I wish I could peel back the years,' but love is timeless and 'my heels broke the soul of the stones' as she allows in a new way of being. In 'We could live in a cwtch of castles. I'll grow my hair' she reflects how, 'I died inside a marriage – I said YES/ to a holy cell and now I lock my life to the pledge/ of my throat. I'm singing!' as the narrator feels herself becoming 'the somewhere sound/ of horses running wild.'

Burn's unbounded imagination makes this an utterly captivating book. Whether she's writing about Covid ('Is Autism/Covid happening to someone/ somewhere else?') when, although she felt 'the happiest I have been for a long while' she starts using predictive text 'to help me show that I care. I am so sorry. I love you.', or writing about birds, such as the dead blackbird she tries to 'cry back alive' ('Poor blackbird crumb'), these poems, like fairytales, take on arrested time. The speaker seems to suggest this, too, when she describes herself as 'the daughter of stopped clocks' ('November's Spoil of Rain and Plague').

Ultimately there is a sense of surrender and acceptance. The closing poem, 'If Ω Is For The Last Thing I Might Ever Do', brings in a prayer-like tone in the words 'Let the sunlight   make a crux gemmata of my plain skin/ crypt the air   with quietus breath'.

Some people turn to poetry for comfort and reassurance, others to be surprised. In *Be Feared* Jane Burn offers both: one woman's honest and inspiring way of coping with the challenges life confronts her with, be it issues of abuse, of food, of having thoughts and desires that diverge from an assumed norm, while at the same time Burn shows how she subverts and transforms her life through poetry that is likely to bewitch the reader with the beauty of its language and imagery.

Mary Mulholland

SK Grout reviews three collections that consider trauma, loss and grief and how poets use language, silence and form to explore these themes

Caroline Bird
Rookie: Selected Poems
Carcanet Press, £12.99

Denise Saul
The Room Between Us
Pavilion Poetry, £9.99

Traian T. Coşovei
Night with a Pocketful of Stones
translated by Adam J. Sorkin & Andreea Iulia Scridon
Broken Sleep Books, £9.99

Rookie: Selected Poems is a selection of ninety-five poems across the past twenty years of Caroline Bird's career from her first collection *Looking Through Letterboxes* in 2002, published at age fifteen, to *The Air Year* in 2020. Half of the collections were written before Bird was twenty-five.

'Geography Lessons' from *Looking Through Letterboxes*, 'and it's all a long walk backwards,/ starting from here', is an intriguing first poem in the ninety-five, given its sense of weighing the future. The collection consists of twelve poems, foundations in Bird's poetics; 'Owl Poem' captures Bird's direct indirectness (direct tone and voice, yet indirect content and subject matter). 'Gingerbread House' and 'Playing at Families' stand out for their surreal and fairy-tale qualities, the poems' abilities to look both ways at once. Preoccupations in this collection are familial relationships and a frustration at the world that sometimes turns to the dramatic. 'I'll break my neck if I jump again from the top of these stairs.' ('I Know this Because You Told Me').

If *Looking Through Letterboxes* explores frustration, in particular, unrequited love, 2006's *Trouble Came to the Turnip* explores violence and sex, including sexual violence. There is more experimentation in this collection; 'An Opera in One Act' plays with operatic tropes and 'Chaining Bikes to this Girl is Strictly Prohibited' functions as a list poem of surreal apology. There are poems of doubling ('Mary-Jane') and extending metaphor and image in 'Shiny Bin', as well as a return to fairy tales, or storytelling, in 'A Seasonal Surprise for Miss Pringle'. In 'My Love Made Me a Hat', violence is held with texture and layering of humour and surrealism: 'A bonnet with a complex.' A reader can sense something terrible through language choice and imagery:

I flap about the yard,
this honey bleeding from my ears,
this terrible, terrible buzzing.
And every day is a summer's day.

The final (titular) poem, 'Trouble Came to the Turnip' moves the reader thematically and stylistically into 2009's *Watering Can*, in which a reader starts to see the crispness and tautness evident in later poems. Every line feels earned. There is more of Bird's signature experimentation this time broadening into form – a villanelle ('Wild Flowers'), a shape poem ('Peaked'), repetition as a poetic device in 'Road Signs', and Bird uses dialogue in these poems to create variety in tone and voice. The violence is there from the previous collection, but it's now simmering under the surface.

'The Monogamy Optician', a few pages earlier, begins a trend that continues in 2012's *The Hat-Stand Union*. Bird extends her use of fairy tales beyond just a device or motif in the poem, into a deeper engagement with modes of narrative. 'A Disgruntled Knight' plays with the idea of who is outside the fairy tale, and 'Mystery Tears' imagines a world where people buy simulated sadness. There is also a process of self-reflection: 'I was treated for fairy-godmother dependency' ('Powerless'). Overwhelmingly, I found Bird using images as a mode of transformation (as in 'The Dry Well' and 'Damage') rather than a container. Poems are more formally experimental such as 'How the Wild Horse Stopped Me', playful as in 'Day Room', and engage with language and sound.

In 'Dry Well', 'You think you know the outcome of the story' utilises Bird's direct voice, but belies the poems' elusive qualities. As earlier, there is a sense of distress and trauma, but it is held in check. As she discusses in her 'Afterword', 'I could take the things I was ashamed of and translate them into dreams, turn drugs into fairy godmothers, breakdowns into tropical islands, depression into a wild horse with a clipboard; and feel protected…'.

Rookie: Selected Poems is rounded off with eighteen poems from 2017's TS Eliot shortlisted *In These Days of Prohibition* and twenty-one poems from 2020's Forward Prize winning *The Air Year*. The former opens with the most direct poem 'A Surreal Joke' as a kind of schism, underlying the gravity of the poem's description of her year in therapy. These are poems that are playful, surreal and funny, still containing the rage, yet in other ways more open, with titles such as 'Bipolar Purgatory', 'Patient Intake Questionnaire' and poems such as 'Stephanie':

Afterwards, my counsellor said
'We really dropped the ball on this one,
placing a sex-addict in a room with a lesbian.'
It'd never occurred to them.

In a similar mode, but completely opposite in content, *The Air Year* opens with a poem about a baby. 'You are the size of an orange seed and/ developing a heart. Same, baby, same.' In 'Primitive Heart', we see Bird's drive to undertake the process of learning and unlearning, which she discussed at the book's launch, thinking about a process of wonder as a process of unlearning. 'A swarm of new questions emerges from every problem they solve. Whatever inspiration is, it's born from a continuous 'I don't know.''[1] From 'The Ground':

You lie and let your bones heal, looking up
at the distance, experiencing plateau
for the first time, cold, hard, real, the opposite of air.

The final poem 'Speechless' opens with 'It is such a relief for the words/ they have been holding so much for so long' as if it's a relief for the speaker, as well as the way they're delivered, and unlike in 'Geography Lessons' where the reader walks backwards from here, the final poem of *Rookie: Selected Poems* climaxes, somewhat uncharacteristically for Bird, with 'life where all business is complete.' Perhaps she is playing with the reader; showing that an ending can also cycle back to a beginning.

For me, *Rookie: Selected Poems* reads like a manifesto. In her launch, Bird talked about carefully curating these poems so that a strong sense of theme would arise; there is certainly doubling, duality, and mirroring as well as the fluidity between the direct and the indirect – a negotiation with truth-telling. Much has been written about fairy tales being a site of queer representation in their mutability and transgression, their ability to look outside the structured path and into the wild forest. Bird also explores the violence and sexual desire within fairy tales. However, I'm intrigued that these poems are listed chronologically and thematically, rather than just thematically – as well as Bird's reasons for choosing 2022 as the right time to release her selected poems. Reading the collection from start to finish does give it a quality of stacking, particularly in the beginning, where the less strong poems stand out. Bird often talks about her willingness to use surrealism as a device to navigate around the truth, so that the collection lies

---

[1] Wisława Szymborska, from 'The poet and the world', Nobel Lecture, December 7, 1996. https://www.nobelprize.org/prizes/literature/1996/szymborska/lecture/

in the reader's hand for their own interpretation, almost like a template. She says in her Afterword: 'Putting this Selected together was the loveliest, luckiest task. And it was also a bit like watching a breakdown in slow motion whilst strapped to a chair.' This is a collection to savour, pore over, read and revisit poems (I could spend the rest of the year learning from the poem titles!) share with friends and fellow poetry lovers, sift out favourites and discuss why.

***

'To study adequately any breakdown in communications we must first understand the nature and structure of the particular mode of communication that has ceased to function. Linguistics is concerned with language in all its aspects – language in operation, language in drift, language in the nascent state, and language in dissolution.' So posits Roman Jakobson in his essay 'Two Aspects of Language and Two Types of Aphasic Disturbances'[2] – a piece of writing that had a large impact on Denise Saul's *The Room Between Us*.

Aphasia is an inability to comprehend or formulate language because of specific damage to the brain. The major causes are stroke and head trauma. The second page in the collection after the titular opening poem appears to be a prose poem with the title 'Stroke' detailing its linguistic explanations. Upon closer inspection to the table of contents, this 'poem' is not listed; it's a rupture in the flow of poems, and very early on.

The Poetry Book Society's 2022 Summer Recommendation *The Room Between Us* grapples with many large-scale life and death questions: how to process and understand the intimacy and spectacle of grief and loss? How to use language to express something without words? How to talk about something that affects a person's ability to use language? Fundamentally, it asks what is language – can the body become language and can language occur in memory if words are not used to describe it?

Saul wants the reader to think considerately about the relationship between caregiver and the person receiving care. This collection allows a window into a private space – between a mother and a daughter, between a carer and a dying person, between loss and grief – and enables the reader to turn these into universal spaces of contemplation.

One way Saul looks at this site of personal-made-universal is through language. But what happens when words have been sundered, as the

---

[2] http://commons.princeton.edu/shakespeares-language/wp-content/uploads/sites/41/2017/09/Jakobson-Two-Aspects-of-Language-and-Two-Types-of-Aphasic-Disturbances.pdf

second page of the collection suggests, by 'a strike', 'a blow'? One of Saul's interests is the role of silence within spaces of trauma and speech disability,[3] the role it plays in expression of language, and in poetry.

Saul uses the form of her poems to consider some of this silence. A number of poems (particularly in the first half) appear as list poems with more white space between lines than text. 'What you leave out is everything. You look away and close your eyes.' ('First Conversation'). The poems that become denser and longer, such as 'The House of Blues', seem to slip from the present-day narrative flow to a space of memory.

Language, and lack of language, is a key part of this collection – and Saul asks us to consider this from the opening poem 'The Room Between Us' which engages with spiritual language (e.g. the Bible), body language and the language of care (hospitals); this then goes on to resonate and appear consistently. The final line of the poem 'now tell me what happened before the fall' is an opening to the speaker, the poet and the reader.

These poems follow a chronology but also engage with memory, moving time and place. Within the care-giving relationship, there is an emphasis on normalcy and routine – 'A representation of a scene is often one simple conversation.' and 'But since my question did not produce an answer, I repeated it.' ('A Daughter's Perspective'). The collection could rupture at the poem 'The Viewing' (seemingly a discussion with a funeral director) which appears in the first half, yet the poems continue embracing specific language, silence, the space of care and the duality of love and loss in grief. 'Even the wheelchair carried her presence in its arm and back.' ('On Sitting').

Most of these poems contain 'she', 'I' or sometimes 'you' – so the roles of mother and daughter, carer and sick person seem blurred. It is possible to read some as inhabiting both spaces at once. Sometimes it's not completely clear who is speaking, and there is a dialogue between and across poems. Particularly startling for me was the poem 'The White Room' about a visit to a doctor; it's unclear who's in the room, just as the timescale is ambiguous to the reader. However, there are ruptures in this way of story-telling and these come in delicately placed detail, as if to use memory to resonate – 'the old tamarind tree' (in 'Apollo Maison Street') or 'long roads of imlah trees' (in 'Lotus Woman'). Saul also uses colour as a recurring motif. The end of the collection, 'a connection with the ways of green/ its part-yellow and part-blue' seems to represent a movement toward healing.

Saul has said in an interview: 'Poetry allows us to explore the difficulties and the challenges of our experiences, and I think that's really

---

[3] https://pentoprint.org/write-on-interviews-writer-denise-saul/

reflected in some of the poems, such as 'A Prayer That May Be Said Before She Wakes' and also with 'A Daughter's Perspective', which explore the challenges of communicating traumatic events.'[4] One of the lines in the latter poem, 'I rub hand-cream into the back of her hand, starting at the wrist and working away from the heart. The nurse told me that it was better to massage away from the heart and not towards it.' reminded me of conversations with nurses for my father's hospice care; a time when lotion on his body would have been a novelty. The relationship between a carer and a sick person can be one of the most intimate of our lives; *The Room Between Us* encourages us to consider how language transforms a personal experience into a universal one.

***

Traian T. Coşovei was a leading Romanian poet of the 80s generation who died in 2014. Son of the poet, Traian Coşovei, he published over twenty books, won a series of prizes including the Prize of the Romanian Academy and the International Nichita Stănescu Prize and was 'undoubtedly one of the purest, most original, and most valuable poets of his generation'.[5] This translation by Adam J. Sorkin and Andreea Iulia Scridon is the first collection published in English.

Coşovei's generation was influenced by 1950s American poets – Coşovei wrote a thesis on the Beat Generation – and there is a sprawling, cascading feel to these poems, an engagement with excess, a broadness spanning the page where words rush down and across. Compellingly, the editors and translators have chosen to feature the poems in both English and Romanian so readers can get a sense, while the words remain mysterious, of the original intent.

Memory is a key theme returned to through the touchstones of photographs, films, statues and dreams. Many poems carry memory as a collective, rather than the singular. 'Lobotomy or Lullaby' is a long poem, that halfway through becomes a list of all things that could be lost after such an operation: 'women/ desires, hopes, psychoanalyses, parliaments'. From 'The Great Photograph':

> Everything's been wiped away
> 　　everything's been forgotten
> 　　　　everything's over, everything

---

[4] https://liverpooluniversitypress.blog/2022/03/16/the-room-between-us-an-interview-with-denise-saul/
[5] Mircea Cărtărescu (Nobel Prize Candidate), from the back cover.

These poems ask: what happens if we lose everything – and what happens next?

With memory, comes the theme of time – but the poet's sense of time is elongated and does not pass quickly. 'The machinery of the century passed over me' and 'I go to bed with this mediaeval moment' ('A Hibernation'). Poems such as 'The Great Photograph', 'Grandfather 'Entre Deux Guerres'' and 'The Accursed Wheel' consider the history of wars and their ramifications across populations, generations, and time. From 'Grandfather 'Entre Deux Guerres'': 'How will you crawl with your knees chopped off// with that hole in your forehead?' From 'The Accursed Wheel': 'I'm afraid to embrace you now/ look, our alarm clock has grown old'.

With these large questions, there is often a sense of melancholy that lingers: 'My dad even sold the water from his well/ to help rescue me from loneliness' ('Requiem').

But this is a broad collection – forty-two poems – and not all face the liminal nor remain in sadness. There are poems of love, anger, comedy – the opening poem is titled 'Bad Boy' – and many are dedicated to loved ones and/or family members. The poem 'Untying the Mast' dedicated 'to Andreea' ends with the beautiful couplet: 'I yearned for an ocean/ to give it your name.'

In one of the book's endorsements, Cosmin Ciotloș writes: 'Coșovei's poetry presents itself as an uninterrupted negotiation. Which means a tension of expression, straining and production. This is where his lyricism emerges. (...) Only rarely has a writer succeeded in balancing in such a nuanced manner the abundant spontaneity of his own language and the constrictive ambition of order.'[6] There is continuous movement in these poems, toward the end of line, the end of the page; poems of brilliance, spontaneity, verve and originality. 'And what if you're an unknown planet?'

The final long poem 'Mickey Mouse is Dead' engages with collective trauma and distress. 'The streets are flesh, are blood, are nerves.' Much of the narrative is spent in the space between life and death, 'Nobody has dreams/ and so I prefer the waiting room', and although neither the eponymous figure of Mickey Mouse nor his death are mentioned in the poem, the reader could consider this poem as living under the regime of Nicolae Ceaușescu (particularly given the number of archive photographs of the dictator at Disneyland).

Translation allows an opportunity to be invited into a time and space that the reader might not otherwise have access to. Much positive change has happened recently with more visibility of the work that translators do,

---

[6] From the back cover

and in their renumeration.[7] It's wonderful to see the names of the translators on the cover of this book, as well as initials on each poem to indicate who translated what. (A full list of translators is also given on the contents page.)

Night with a Pocketful of Stones includes neither foreword nor afterword and does not indicate from which collections each poem comes in the section breaks. On the one hand, this allows the reader to meet the poems on the page – there is a face-to-face conversation, we can enjoy and resonate with the language, imagery and worlds being built, without preconceptions of another voice summarising, directing the reader as to how to read or interpret the poems. The only filter is that of the poet (and translators). On the other hand, this means limited context is provided: when or where the poems were written, and on what timeline. It's difficult to understand the poet's oeuvre as it's not indicated if the poems are collected chronologically (after all, there are twenty books of his work). For a first meeting in the English language, this does feel like a missed opportunity; it puts more onus on the reader to do the research. That's not necessarily a bad thing, but here's hoping that this collection stimulates more interest in this very important poet.

SK Grout

---

[7] Jennifer L. Croft, 'Why translators should be named on book covers', *The Guardian*, September 10, 2021 https://www.theguardian.com/books/2021/sep/10/why-translators-should-be-named-on-book-covers and Society of Authors, Translators on the Cover, Open Letter https://www2.societyofauthors.org/translators-on-the-cover/

Reviews in Brief edited by Mary Mulholland

Eds. Al Filreis and Anna Strong Safford
The Difference Is Spreading, fifty contemporary poets on fifty poems
University of Pennsylvania Press, £22.99

Keen readers of poetry will be pleased to discover this inspiring and insightful book whose origins stem from an online course exploring modern American Poetry, started in 2012 and hosted by the Kelly Writers House at University of Pennsylvania.[8]

The most engaging poems are never fully understood but invite the reader to participate in a deepening appreciation. This book does exactly that. As the editors state in their introduction, 'interpretation stands as never more than an opening'. Tracie Morris describes the book as a 'paginated, welcoming dinner party.'

The title is taken from Gertrude Stein's 'A Carafe, that is a Blind Glass', which Ron Silliman discusses in his essay evaluating the debt modern poets still owe to Stein. Stein's daring forays into ambiguity and deconstruction of language also influenced her contemporary, William Carlos Williams. 'Stein [...] got there first.' writes Silliman, requiring the reader to be fully present to language and to how each word connects.

The poets writing about other poets are additionally authors, editors and professors and include Rae Armantrout, Charles Bernstein, Christian Bok, Lyn Hejinian and Bernadette Mayer. Though some poems discussed may be well known, such as Sylvia Plath's 'Lady Lazarus', John Ashbery's 'Just Walking Around', and Gwendolyn Brooks's 'Boy Breaking Glass' there's always occasion for new thought.

In her analysis of Frank O'Hara's 'Poem (Khrushchev is coming on the right day)' Marjorie Perloff (professor at Stanford and University of Southern California) reminds the reader how subtly politics is present as the narrator breezes through his day recollecting comments made by his art circle, and, by fusing his private life with public happenings, hints at the fragility of life. O'Hara's line 'where does the evil of the year go/ when September takes New York' is a chilling reminder that nothing can be taken for granted.

Whether contextualising a poem, or lingering in its soundscape, as Bernstein says in his thoughts on Hejinian, 'There's more to a poem than blue cheese.' One of the joys of reading poetry is unpacking it, like a parcel with many wrappings. I'd recommend this book to any poet who enjoys delving deep.

---

[8] https://modpo.org/category/kellywritershouse/

Sarah Wimbush
Shelling Peas with My Grandmother in the Gorgiolands
Bloodaxe, £10.99

The opening poem, 'House' immediately caught my attention: 'the first time/ I went into a house/ there were so many rooms', highlighting a way of life non-travellers take for granted. There have been several books exploring the Romany life recently, but Wimbush's insights include a particularly fascinating account of early childhood memories.

In 'Mother Tongue' she shares Romani words, such as '*Dukker* is to see/ the future or your fortune,' and the word also appears in 'Carroty Kate': 'I get by dukkering at the net marketplace –'. The poet reveals herbal remedies, 'a dandelion sap or well-hung pork fat/ works like magic on warts and moles' in 'Gran Violet Applies a Poultice', while in 'The Bittern' she recalls 'wintering-over/ in two-up two-down cottage' for home-schooling and hearing the bittern 'like a breath blown over a bottle. On a still day, I feel that call for miles.' What strongly comes across is both Wimbush's pride for a people who are part of the land, and her generosity in sharing.

'White Cottage' tells of women who 'pulled their own teeth', who 'didn't exist on paper, and yet, could recite the name/ of every pea field she'd ever worked through'. The title poem is a riveting list of Romany warnings: 'never tell anyone/ when the visions come' and 'mind when to leave the book of your mouth open/ when to fold it into a crossed knife.'

The poem, 'Census 1911' is a shocking revelation of the historical attitude towards a community barely recognised by the state:

> On the census, Annie (Fanny)
> and young Tommy
> are not learning to hawk
> and trap small game, respectively -
> they go to school.

The poet's later personal experiences show a more 'integrated' way of life with humorous recall, as in 'Inside Lingerie' where 'the husband who stands poker-straight, arms folded,/ next to the scarlet push-me-up jj cups.' Members of the poet's family went down the mines and Wimbush writes movingly in 'The Lost' about 'the seven lads who never came back'.

The closing poem, 'Our Language', is a celebration: 'our language still exists. It roars by gas fires, and at the far table in the Club and in the living museum beside the image of a man digging forever through a coal seam two foot thick.' This is a captivating collection offering important insights into a way of life perhaps previously little-known or understood.

Helen Quah
Dog Woman
Out-Spoken Press, £7

The epigraph for this debut pamphlet is taken from Li-Young Lee, who uses the personal to explore the universal, while the title poem is taken from a Paula Rego painting; Rego used art to challenge (among other things) stereotyped attitudes towards women. There is an echo of this theme in the poems by Helen Quah, a British poet of Guyanese and Chinese-Malaysian descent, who is also a junior doctor, as she explores her experience of being a modern, mixed-race working woman.

The second poem of the book, 'Suburbia', begins: 'Women are auditioning to be themselves', highlighting the narrator's search for identity, alongside an awareness that 'We all have shit to carry.' The poem concludes 'Women can make the same sound/ as a wolf, and they do.' Wolf is one of many animal references employed by the poet, perhaps evoking the idea of women connecting to their animal natures.

As with Rego's art, some images are strange and unsettling. In 'Dog Woman' Quah writes, 'They ride horses, eat lettuce,/ have abortions on leather sofas,' which creates a sense of aloneness and trauma, of being objectified which is also conveyed in 'We don't look for comfort' when the poet writes: 'I am made completely/ of empty promises'. This poem describes an incident when two sisters of 11 and 15, walking in Soho were mistaken for masseuses. 'I still rub my belly/ when in distress'. The poem ends with the surreal image: 'we take off our feet/ unclipped at the ankle'.

For Quah, issues of racial identity and oppression are ever-present. In the third of her series '[When I Marry a White Man]', the poet writes 'I'm made of stains and hiccups', while the fourth section contains the lines: 'I've emptied all kindness/ from its fact', concluding: 'Pour over/ my own slab half myself awake/ more brutal than before.'

The emotional contradictions inherent in mother/daughter relationships are movingly captured in 'Fifteen minutes' (after Kim Hyesoon), where the narrator imagines her mother's death, 'You will fight with her like in life', and while 'The dead leaving the dead was not something that troubles you' Quah concludes that 'Your breasts ache as she sits downstairs alone, laughing with the television'.

This is an absorbing, arresting, sometimes disturbing pamphlet.

Sarah Mnatzaganian
Lemonade in the Armenian Quarter
Against the Grain, £6

This warming debut pamphlet reads like a book of gratitude, tenderly weaving strands of identity and culture as the poet reflects upon her Armenian-British heritage.

The poems are dotted with place names, from Normandy to Palestine and Jerusalem to Hemsworth, together with family members' names, from the speaker's parents to Uncle Hagop, Auntie Merhibeh, Ursula, Miriam and others. It's as if the reader is a guest in their lives.

Mouthwatering smells and tastes are included in many of the poems – cardamon coffee, baklava, lahmajoun, ma'loubeh, babaghanous, labane, fresh yellow dates. The title, 'In Praise of Armenian Cooks', seems to pay tribute to this, and in 'Green Valley Supermarket', the poet highlights the importance of food to both culture and family as she tells staff that her father

> taught Arabic
> to the owner's sons, but they don't understand.
> I want them to know I'm here to buy
> the flavours of my father's childhood.

English apples also put in an appearance: 'Blenheim Orange, Winter Gold' as an apple and almond cake is cooked and posted to family members, irrespective of cost. This seems to suggest a parallel between blending ingredients and nationalities.

The warmth with which family personalities are described is particularly poignant in 'Father Tree' where the narrator depicts her father's hand 'thrust into the earth, each finger reaching/ for Palestine, seeking his mother's bones,' as he undergoes a (successful) operation, possibly for a DVT, the same that had killed his own mother.

There is gratitude, too, for the freedom of being in a country where, for all its shortcomings, 'all the birds are welcome here/ whatever language they speak'. In 'Morning' with its echo of mourning for the grandmother who didn't survive, the poet writes: 'I would give this morning to those I don't even love'.

Another theme which seems to run through the pamphlet is the speaker's recognition of a need to be part of a wider world. In 'Araxi, 85', a daughter is 'pale with jetlag and a migrant's guilt' while elsewhere she writes, 'I will not be afraid when she walks away, for as long as it takes to leave'. These poems are a gentle, uplifting read.

Richard Skinner
Dream into Play
Poetry Salzburg, £7.50

This is a densely-packed pamphlet to reread and savour. Skinner's lyrical poems brim with his trademark intertextuality, intelligence and wit. The title could well be a take on Strindberg's *A Dream Play*, which challenges Nietzsche's philosophy of eternal recurrence. Skinner's poems seem infused with Eastern philosophy and consider the transient nature of reality/ dream/ illusion, as in '*the deer*': 'She bolted and, quick as life,/was gone.' The final poem leaves the reader with the question of 'What to hold on to' ('Life in a Oncetime'). In 'Black Objects' 'I am praying for a belief in uncertainty'.

Though sometimes dealing with abstract ideas, the poems are rooted in materiality of the poet's emotional and personal experiences. In the opening poem, 'The Green Capitals' the narrator powerfully recalls 'that last time your mother stopped/ you dead in your tracks with her truth', and references 'a tear in a broken heart', while 'her words' are 'echoing in the room/ that everyone carries inside them.' The theme of the nature of truth seems to continue in the second poem, dedicated to the poet's father, where it is set alongside the slippery word 'lies': 'the truth a poem emplaces/ often lies in its pattern.'

In 'Atropos', one of the three fates, Skinner's explorations go deeper, asserting 'the illusory is always a part of reality'. The poet writes: 'any description of the world that omits our dreams/ would only be a dream'.

In his sequence on how photography can alter 'reality', he writes, 'This is not/ the real world.' ('A Patch of Birch'). Perhaps only emotions are real, yet they too shift. In 'Caedmon's Hymn', 'grief is nothing but a release of love', and in 'The Real Star', the speaker writes movingly of 'all the hurt, unsaid, never/ solved, lapping up on some distant shore.'

Skinner counters his philosophies with witty wordplay, such as 'Crocodile Mother', where the words 'tears' and 'mothers' are interchanged: 'Blood sweat and mother. The tears of all battles.'... 'It will all end in mother.' Another favourite was 'Poems in the restroom':

Poem Rolls 2
Sit in a relaxed position with your poem at your side. Slowly roll your poem forward five times. Reverse the motion and repeat five times.

Skinner's poems explore the nature of what makes up our individual worlds and 'how not to mix the good water with the bad.' ('Ken/ Keeping Still, Mountain'), hinting at living mindfully and questioningly. In 'Black Objects', he writes: 'If you don't sleep, someone else will steal all your dreams.' This pamphlet is likely to become a personal favourite.

Anita Pati
Hiding to Nothing
Liverpool University Press, £9.99

This debut collection is a welcome follow-on from the poet's pamphlet, *Dodo Provocateur*. Pati explores the legacy of empire and experiences of being othered, both in terms of race and as a woman, on subsequent generations.

In 'She's in stocks, and shares' the poet seems to be both the fish and one of the group handling the fish, perhaps to reflect the destabilising effects of displacement: 'when she was filleted/ and each piece packaged in dainty foils/ bowed with taffeta, we settled her', and the disinterested, blunt ending 'when she shrivelled, we sold her and that was that.'

There are disquieting nursery tale references, such as the three little pigs, or images Pati herself creates: 'One day the townsfolk ate the white meat of her irises/ with a dessert fork [...] Because she was a witch they grew back.' And violence, 'In Manju': 'She'd take his whipping/ always again/ on her keloid skin', while 'The Girl Who Would Be King' brought Daljit Nagra's *Look we have coming to Dover* to my mind. There is also much tenderness and grief. In 'NoMo' the poet writes: 'I don't want to do this to myself', foreshadowing difficulties around motherhood, and there's a loving reference to 'Our little butterbean'.

I missed the presence of a contents page, as Pati's titles are compelling, such as 'Paperdolls/ *or*/ Where Are My Curly Scrolls of Sisters' and it would have been good to see them together, but possibly this was because the central section takes the unusual form of fragments of interviews, left or right margined, sometimes in bold, capitalised, mostly untitled, under the umbrella title, 'Bloodfruit'.

In this section connections between 'unbelonging' and body-image are explored, with particular emphasis on motherhood, infertility and premature birth. Some of the interview fragments are heart-breaking, like the five-times repeated '**I was miscarrying perfect embryos** and they couldn't stop'; 'I would give/ anything/ to not have this'; and another line, '**I could never mother another like she mothered me, never.**/ That's why some of us don't mother.'

One poem I found particularly moving was 'Her World Is Fury', towards the end of the book. Its unusual capitalisation of 'Her' highlighted the force of the striking images, such as 'the heart/ of Her is a bruise waiting bee-sting' and 'Her, whose wrath comes in thunder's four-second delay.'

This lyrical first collection explores ideas around self-worth and unbelonging in dazzling brave and powerful poems using a multitude of innovative and exciting forms.

Phoebe Power
Book of Days
Carcanet, £11.99

Described as part-memoir, part-meditation on community and spirituality, Phoebe Power's second collection recounts a journey along the Camino pilgrimage to Santiago de Compostela.

The journey starts in Ely Cathedral when the speaker seems to be questioning her own belief system followed by a chance encounter with a nun who gives her a book of her memoirs. At once the reader is on pilgrimage, alongside the narrator, crammed in dormitories, communally eating in church halls, walking, walking, with all conversations starting mid-sentence.

'At Orisson, everyone's American, long-legged, crammed/ around with beers. [...] Clare says, this isn't exactly peace and time to think.' 'My mum's here with me. You can't see her, but she's here.' 'I'm carrying Dad's ashes', 'I don't know the reason yet but I will.'

There are very many names of people met along the journey, Courtney, Em, Rachel, Matt. 'All set off together, start in the same grey promise. Walking in one irregular string' to the sound of 'Cattle bells'. 'We stop on the path./ Do you mind if I pray for you, real quick.' Then, afterwards, 'when she's done, we hug/ I'm crying'.

The open sharing of the Camino is reflected in the innovative way Power lets the 'I' dominate in multiple voices, so it is never clear who is speaking, rather a sense is created of being on the journey together with 'The crowds of heavy-necked souls, climbing/ Purgatory mountain' with their 'currency of kindness', and 'The evening the colour of meat and Ciara's dyed hair'.

Map readers might enjoy following the right-margined place names, such as *Puente la Reina, Lorca.*

The pilgrims' concerns centre on hair-conditioner, blisters, food, and how far they will walk; 'I guess I still don't know where I'm going, but I saw I had to leave.' There seems to be something almost addictive about the pilgrimage: 'After I finished the walk, I came back. I usually stay a few months... actually I hate it.' 'Every hundred yards or so, Rachel/ skips forwards, builds a cairn.'

Stylistically, delicate poems intersperse prosier sections, such as, at *Tosantos*,

> clutches of black
> berries, thistles
> and burgundy gorse

But lest the reader misread any apparently naive comments, Power writes:

> *and none of it is masquerade*
> *and all of it is truth*
> *and no one is scared to say*
> *and all of us are safe here*

Did Power find her answer? She never shared her question. The epilogue returns to the narrator and her appointment mentioned at the start, with 'James', who may be the speaker's pastoral tutor. It also remains unclear whose pilgrimage we read about. Power's? the nun's? everyman's? Does it matter? It is still a fine read.

Gillie Robic
Open Skies
Live Canon, £7

This timely pamphlet of poems reminding us of the devastation of war and dedicated 'to the lost' is donating its proceeds to the Ukrainian Institute's fundraiser to provide English lessons to Ukrainians resettled in the UK. Robic's poems are lyrical and wry. They invite the reader to consider human action and the world humans are creating. In 'war offices'

> *i. ministry of food*
>
> he likes a bloomer
> she artisan sourdough
> the displaced want bread

The poems are not specifically about the war in Ukraine, but also celebrate the light, and consider post-apocalyptic times. 'Guano Inc' has a humorous take on this: 'We're good tenants, we've reserved/ the Executive Toilets for our rich deposits'. In 'the turning'

> see how some miss the moment of turning
> sucked in the undertow of the fall
> cancelling hope concussion of darkness
> coffined within the day's brief light

The speaker looks skyward as she places humans in context of the universe and considers 'How it ends': 'The sun explodes. Well, that's what it's always doing,' and the ending of this poem carries a sense of the poet's personal despair at human failure to learn from the past: 'Automatic feet trample the cosmos, pulverise the whole exhausted galaxy.' These poems are powerful and subtle, for example, the closing poem's title contains the colours of the Ukrainian flag 'skyblue sungold', 'psalmody across the earth/ never pause for death'.

Contributors

Simon Alderwick is originally from England but has spent most of the last eight years in the Philippines. His poetry has recently appeared in *Acropolis, Magma, Dust, Ink Sweat & Tears, Acid Bath, Cape, The Telegraph, Impractical Things* and *InkDrinkers*, among others.

Caroline Bird is a poet, playwright and performer whose seventh collection, *Rookie, Selected Poems,* came out this summer with Carcanet. Her previous six collections, all with Carcanet, include *In these Days of Prohibition,* 2017, which was shortlisted for both the TS Eliot and Ted Hughes Award, and *The Air Year,* 2020, which won the Forward Prize. www.carolinebird.co.uk

Frank Brunner teaches physics in the Adirondack Mountains, where he lives with his wife, children, and a giant Newfoundland dog. The Newfie occasionally accompanies Frank into the classroom and does a spectacular job of demonstrating inertia. Frank's poetry has appeared in *Mobius, Pulsebeat Poetry, Fiery Scribe*, and elsewhere.

Diana Cant is a child psychotherapist with an MA in Poetry from Newcastle University/The Poetry School. Her poems have been published in various anthologies and magazines, and she was voted the Canterbury People's Poet in 2021. Her pamphlet, *Student Bodies 1968*, was published in 2020 by Clayhanger Press, and her second pamphlet, *At Risk – the lives some children live*, was published by Dempsey and Windle in 2021.

Sam Bootle is an Associate Professor of French Literature at Durham University, specialising in late nineteenth-century French poetry. He has published a book on the poet Jules Laforgue, and is currently working on translations of Laforgue's *Derniers Vers*, as well as writing his own poetry.

Ken Cockburn is a poet and translator based in Edinburgh. After several years at the Scottish Poetry Library, since 2004 he has freelanced, working in education, care and community settings, often collaborating with visual artists. His most recent collection is *Floating the Woods* (Luath, 2018). https://kencockburn.co.uk

Tamsin Cottis is a child psychotherapist and writer of short fiction and poetry, Tamsin's work has been placed or long/shortlisted for several short story prizes including *Mslexia, Fish, Bath* and *London*. Tamsin has been published by, among others, *The Mechanics Institute Review, FlashBackFiction, Rattle Tales, Peepal Press, Atrium*, and *Verve*.

Janet Dean was brought up in a mining community in South Yorkshire. After a forty-year career in public service she completed an MA in Creative Writing in 2015. Shortlisted for the Bridport Prize, her work appears widely in magazines and anthologies and in the Northern Poetry Library.

Alexander Etheridge has been developing his poems and translations since 1998. His poems have been featured in *Scissors and Spackle, Ink Sac, Cerasus Journal, The Cafe Review, The Madrigal, Abridged Magazine, Susurrus Magazine, The Journal,* and many others. He was the winner of the Struck Match Poetry Prize in 1999.

Pascal Fallas is a writer and (occasional) photographer currently living in Norfolk. His poems have recently appeared in *Ink, Sweat and Tears, London Grip, The Fenland Poetry Journal, Brittlestar* and *The Alchemy Spoon.* To contact or for more information please visit www.pascalfallas.com.

Al Filreis is Kelly Professor of English, Faculty Director of the Kelly Writers House, Director of the Center for Programs in Contemporary Writing, Co-Director of PennSound, Publisher of *Jacket2* magazine—all at the University of Pennsylvania, where he has been a member of the faculty since 1985.

Miles Gibson runs a small farm in west Oxfordshire growing fruit which he makes into liqueurs. He also keeps his hand in as a psychotherapist. Shortly after his 50th birthday he began writing poetry and attending Zoom workshops at CityLit. He has had poems published in *South Bank Magazine.*

SK Grout is an editor and writer who grew up in Aotearoa, New Zealand, lived in Germany and now splits her time between London and Auckland Tāmaki Makaurau. Her debut chapbook, *What love would smell like,* was published by V. Press in 2021. https://skgroutpoetry.wixsite.com/poetry.

Chris Hardy has travelled widely. After years in London he lives in Sussex. His poems have been published in magazines, anthologies, online, and have been highly commended and shortlisted in the Poetry Society, Live Canon and other competitions. Chris's new collection *Key to the Highway* is published by Shoestring Press.

Alex Harford enjoys photography, art and writing (in all sorts of genres), as well as visiting places that don't seem real, the outdoors, reading (mostly flash and fantasy short stories), films, and music. He can occasionally be seen in his microlight, vacuuming and redistributing clouds. https://AlexHarford.uk

Doryn Herbst is a former scientist in Wales, now lives in Germany. Her writing considers the natural world but also themes which address social issues. Doryn has poetry in *Fahmidan Journal*, *The Dirigible Balloon*, *CERASUS Magazine*, *Fenland Poetry Journal* and more. She is a reviewer at *Consilience* science poetry journal.

CJ House is a poet creating works about the world and their life.

Dawn Jutton is an artist with an eclectic practice that often crosses genre boundaries and is usually inspired by heritage and landscape. Her mild obsession with teasing out new connections from often forgotten or carelessly discarded objects is underpinned by skills developed during her early career as a studio photographer at Wedgwood.

Peter Kenny writes poems, plays and prose. He co-hosts www.planetpoetrypodcast.com with Robin Houghton. Poetry publications include *Sin Cycle* (e.ratio, 2020) *The Nightwork* (Telltale Press, 2014) and *A Guernsey Double* (Guernsey Arts Commission, 2010). He blogs at peterkenny.co.uk

Janet Lancaster is Welsh by birth and grew up in South Wales. She is a married, retired teacher of Modern Languages and lives in Rutland. She has an MA (Creative Writing - Poetry) MMU, 2010. Her poems have been published in anthologies and the Poetry Society website Stanza Competition pages. Her interests include contemporary poetry, family history, travel, walking and archery.

Sue Lewis is a South London poet who began reading and writing poetry as a way of finding her voice and confidence after a mid-life stroke. She has twice won the Cinnamon Press Pamphlet Award: in 2019 with *Texture*; and again in 2021 with *Journey* (published in March 2022).

Tim Love's publications are a poetry pamphlet *Moving Parts* (HappenStance) and a story collection *By all means* (Nine Arches Press). He lives in Cambridge, UK. His poetry and prose have appeared in *Stand*, *Rialto*, *Magma*, *Unthology*, etc. He blogs at http://litrefs.blogspot.com/

Jane Lovell's work focuses on our relationship with the planet and its wildlife. She recently won the Ginkgo Prize and Rialto/RSPB Nature & Place Competition. *The God of Lost Ways* and *This Tilting Earth* are her latest eco-poetry publications.

Fokkina McDonnell has two poetry collections (Oversteps Books; Indigo Dreams Publishing) and a pamphlet (Grey Hen Press, 2020). Poems have been widely published and anthologized. She received a Northern Writers' Award from New Writing North in 2020 for *Remembering/Disease*. Broken Sleep Books will publish the collection in late 2022.

James McDermott's poetry collection *Manatomy*, longlisted for Polari's First Book Prize 2021, is published by Burning Eye and their pamphlet *Erased* is published by Polari Press. James's pamphlet of queer nature poems, *Green Apple Red*, is forthcoming with Broken Sleep Books.

Karen Macfarlane lives in Perthshire. She is an Occupational Therapist and mid-life Arts & Humanities student. Her poems have appeared in *Poetry Scotland*, *Gallus* and *Spelt Magazine*. She won third place in the Scottish Mountain Writing competition 2020.

Jennifer A. McGowan took her PhD from the University of Wales. Arachne Press will publish her sixth collection in October 2022. She spends as much time as she can in the 15th century, rather than the 21st.

Annie Morris lives in SW London. Her poems have appeared in various online and print publications such as *Minute Magazine*, *Allegro*, *Red Wolf Journal*, *Blue Heron Review*, *The Dawntreader*, *Shot Glass Journal*, *Amethyst Review* and the anthology *Myth & Metamorphosis* (Penteract Press).

Jeri Onitskansky is a 61-year-old Jungian analyst and poet. Her poems have been published widely. She won the 2012 Ledbury and 2019 Ver Poets competitions. Her pamphlet *Call them Juneberries* (Templar Poetry) won the iOTA shot award. Her debut collection, *Kayaköy*, is forthcoming in January 2023 with Blue Diode Press.

Kate Oldfield has worked in non-fiction publishing for 25 years. During lockdown, she resurrected a poetry journal kept before university. She challenged herself to write a poem a week and, in doing so, reawakened a passion for poetry. She lives in Oxford with her long-suffering audience: two teens, two cats.

Tim Relf's poems have appeared in *Acumen*, *The Rialto*, *The Frogmore Papers*, *Poetry Salzburg*, *Wild Court*, *One Hand Clapping*, *Ink Sweat & Tears* and *The Friday Poem*. He is an alumnus of Faber's Advanced Poetry Academy 2021/2022. His most recent novel, *What She Left*, was published by Penguin.

Mary Robinson's first collection, *The Art of Gardening* (Flambard, 2010), was published in her 60th year. Recent work includes a pamphlet, *Alphabet Poems* (Mariscat, 2019), and a second collection, *Trace* (Oversteps, 2020). Her poetry has been published in several magazines. She lives in North Wales.

Bridget Ramsey retired in 2020 after happy years teaching writing and literature to middle and high school students in Colorado, Virginia, New Orleans, and Florida. She recently began an MFA program, writes daily, reads, plays tennis, and enjoys the bounty of living near the ocean and spending time with cherished ones.

Catherine Redford lives in the West Midlands. She began writing poetry after being widowed at the age of 35. She has poems published or forthcoming in *New Welsh Reader*, *Black Bough Poetry*, *Atrium*, *Green Ink Poetry*, *Dear Reader*, and *The Banshee*. Twitter: @C_Redford_

Martin Rieser is a poet /artist. He is widely published, including *Poetry Review*, *Write to be Counted*, *Magma* and *Morphrog 22*. He was shortlisted for Frosted Fire 2019 /2022 and the Charles Causeley Prize 2020 as well as runner up in the Norman Nicholson 2020. He won the Hastings Poetry Competition 2021and runs the Stanza Bristol.

Geoff Sawers' previous collections include *Scissors Cut Rock* (Flarestack, 2005) and *A Thames Bestiary* with Peter Hay (Two Rivers Press, 2008); he has also written several non-fiction books. Born in 1966, he was only diagnosed as autistic in his fifties.

Sue Wallace-Shaddad has an MA from Newcastle University. Dempsey & Windle published her pamphlet, *A City Waking Up*, October 2020. Shortlisted for the 2021 Plough Prize, her poems feature in many online and print publications. Sue writes poetry reviews and is secretary of Suffolk Poetry Society. https://suewallaceshaddad.wordpress.com

Lesley Sharpe teaches literature and creative writing, and edits Heron journal for the Katherine Mansfield Society. Her poems and essays have been published in several journals and anthologies and been short- and long-listed for prizes including The London Magazine, Aesthetica, Cinnamon Debut Collection and Bridport.

Jeffery Sugarman is an American-born poet in London. He was a 2019 Jerwood/Arvon mentee with Hannah Lowe and is published in *Present Tense*, *Magma*, and *Finished Creatures*; his debut chapbook, *Dear Friend(s)*, explores kinship and loss, particularly during the early AIDS epidemic of the 1990s, available from The Emma Press.

Laura Theis's work appears in *Poetry*, *Mslexia*, *Rattle*, etc. A Forward Prize nominee and AM-Heath-Prize recipient, she won the Oxford Brookes Poetry Prize, Mogford Prize, Hammond House Literary Award, and was a finalist for the National Poetry Competition. Her debut *how to extricate yourself* won the Brian Dempsey Memorial Prize.

Phil Vernon has published two collections: *Poetry After Auschwitz* (Sentinel, 2020) and *Watching the Moon Landing* (Hedgehog, 2022). His *Stabat Mater*, with music by Nicola Burnett Smith, has been performed in the UK and abroad. He is writing a collection on the links between peace, conflict and place, *Guerrilla Country*.

Marian de Vooght was born in the Netherlands and moved to Austin, Texas, to do a PhD in Comparative Literature. After that she taught at universities in Norway, Germany, and the UK. She translates poetry and is co-editor of *Poetry of the Holocaust: An Anthology* (Arc Publications, 2019).

Dennis Williams is an emerging poet/writer from Sandy Hill, St. Catherine, Jamaica. His inaugural poem, 'They burn the city', was published in the *Agape Review*.

Alexandra Williams is a copywriter from London who lives near Newbury, Berkshire. She turned her hand to poetry two years ago and has recently published work in *Door Is A Jar*, *Brave Voices* and The Minison Project's *TMP Magazine*.

Pat Winslow worked as an actor before leaving theatre in 1987. She's published seven poetry collections, including *Kissing Bones* and *Unpredictable Geometry* with Templar Poetry. Pat recently discovered time = space in the Outer Hebrides when she was working on a novel. She looks forward to having more.

Marjory Woodfield's prose, poetry and articles have appeared in *The BBC*, stuff.co.nz; *Orbis*, *Pennine Platform*, *The Lake* and in *Pale Moon*, (Frogmore Press), *Best Short Fiction* (Sonder Press). She won The New Zealand Robert Burns Competition and has been placed in Hippocrates, Yeovil, Ver and John McGivering writing competitions.

Judith Wozniak has an MA in Writing Poetry from The Poetry School and Newcastle University. Her poems have recently appeared in, *South*, *The Alchemy Spoon*, *Fenland Poetry Journal*, *The Frogmore Papers*, *London Grip* and *These are the Hands NHS Anthology*. She won first prize in the Hippocrates Competition 2020.

Martin Yates was born on Merseyside, raised in the Black Country and now lives and works in the West Midlands. He recently gained an MA in Creative Writing from Birmingham City University. His work has appeared in *The Rialto*, *Stand*, *Poetry Wales*, *Finished Creatures* and *Butcher's Dog*.

Submission Guidelines

We welcome submissions of up to three brilliant, unpublished, original poems on the issue's theme through the website during the submission window. You will find full details of how to submit on our website: www.alchemyspoon.org.

We are only able to accept submissions from those over 18.

If you have poems published in the current issue of *The Alchemy Spoon*, then we ask that you wait out one issue before submitting more work.

Simultaneous submissions are permitted but please tell us straightaway if a poem is accepted for publication elsewhere.

We aim for a speedy turn-round and will respond to every submission, but we don't offer individual feedback.

Authors retain all rights. However, if a poem is then published elsewhere, please acknowledge that it first appeared in *The Alchemy Spoon*.

Our submission window for Issue 8 will be open 1st–31st October 2022, the theme for the issue will be 'Gift' and we will welcome poems on this theme up to 40 lines. See our website for the full details.

Submission Guidelines for Essays
If you have an essay on some cutting-edge poetry-related topic, please send it to us during the submission window for consideration +/- 1500 words.

Submission Guidelines for Artwork
We are always looking for original artwork to feature on future magazine covers. Portrait-orientated images work best (or images suitable for cropping). Good quality lower resolution images can be sent at the submission stage, but higher res files will be needed (2480 pixels x 3508 pixels) at print stage.

Submission Guidelines for Reviews
If you would like to recommend a poetry collection or submit a review of a collection, then please email us or use the contact form on the website.

Poetry Workshops
The Alchemy Spoon editors offer a one-to-one poetry feedback and workshopping service without prejudice via Zoom or Facetime. All profits from this contribute to the cost of running Clayhanger Press. Please email vanessa.tas@btinternet.com to arrange this.

Cover Design by Clayhanger Press

Typesetting and Design Roger Bloor
Senior Copy Editor Sara Levy
Proof-reader Adam Lampert

www.clayhangerpress.co.uk

Clayhanger Press

Printed in Great Britain
by Amazon

85238424R00066